# THE CHRISTIAN PASTOR

# THE CHRISTIAN PASTOR
## THE OFFICE AND DUTY
## OF THE GOSPEL MINISTER

LECTURES DELIVERED AT
BOSTON UNIVERSITY
SCHOOL OF THEOLOGY
SEPTEMBER 29 – OCTOBER 3, 1873

## STEPHEN H. TYNG

Solid Ground Christian Books
Birmingham, Alabama USA

Solid Ground Christian Books
2090 Columbiana Rd, Suite 2000
Birmingham, AL 35216
205-443-0311
sgcb@charter.net
http://solid-ground-books.com

**THE CHRISTIAN PASTOR**
**The Office and Duty of the Gospel Minister**

Stephen H. Tyng (1800-1885)

*Solid Ground Classic Reprints*

First edition March 2006

Taken from 1874 edition by Harper & Brothers, Franklin Square, NY

Cover work by Borgo Design, Tuscaloosa, AL
Contact them at nelbrown@comcast.net

*Cover image is of a lone shepherd surveying his flock in Magellanes State
in southern Chile. ©Ric Ergenbright. Special thanks to Ric for permission
to use this image. Go to ricergenbright.com to view his photographs.*

1-59925-055-1

# Explanation for This Book

Stephen H. Tyng (1800-1885) had been in the Gospel Ministry over 50 years when he was asked by the School of Theology in Boston University to deliver a lectureship on *The Christian Pastor* to the men who were training for the work of the ministry. The contents of this book are the results of that assignment. Tyng had no intention of putting these lectures into print until he received the following encouragements from both the student body and the faculty. In his own words:

"I should scarce feel at liberty to append the following resolutions and personal expressions of esteem and honor, if it did not appear to me ungrateful and disrespectful to omit them, excessive as I feel them to be in their relation to myself. They are the separate action of the students and the faculty of the Theological School in the Boston University, received with the request for the publication which I have now made."

BOSTON UNIVERSITY,
SCHOOL OF THEOLOGY,
October 3, 1873.

REV. STEPHEN H. TYNG, D.D.

Dear Sir,—As a committee of the students, we desire to express the deep interest we have felt while listening to your recent lectures before us upon the Christian pastorate. And we earnestly request, if it be your pleasure, that they may be published, both for our future study and for the edification of our brethren in the ministry.
Respectfully,

A COMITTEE FROM THE STUDENTS.

"A short time later I received the following from the distinguished faculty:"

# RESOLUTIONS
## PASSED BY THE FACULTY OF THE SCHOOL OF THEOLOGY IN BOSTON UNIVERSITY.

It is encouraging, refreshing, and ennobling to meet one whose keen intellectual perceptions appear not to have been in the least blunted, but rather improved with his advancing years; the pureness and chasteness of whose language, and the simplicity of whose style, throw a rich charm over every sentence used; and whose affectionate devotion to his Lord and Master is the sweetest and most perfect charm of all;

Therefore Resolved, That we, the Faculty of the School of Theology, Boston University, extend our sincere thanks to the Rev. Dr. Tyng for his excellent lectures upon "The Pastoral Office;" which have been characterized with the sharp discrimination of a professed dialectician; with the rhetorical excellence of one who is a master of his mother-tongue; and with the earnestness of one whose soul is alive to the grandest interests of the REDEEMER'S KINGDOM.

Also Resolved, That we recognize in Dr. Tyng one who for more than half a century has faithfully and successfully fulfilled the duties of that office, with whose importance and dignity he has so deeply impressed us.

And also Resolved, That in our judgment Dr. Tyng will render the Church and the ministry a lasting service by allowing the publication of his admirable lectures.

Having read over this volume several times during the process of editing, we are convinced that this generation desperately needs this work, and we are both delighted and honored to introduce it once again. May the Lord Jesus Christ, the Great and Good Shepherd of the sheep, use this volume to stimulate the brethren to love and good works.

THE PUBLISHER
FEBRUARY 28, 2006

# TABLE OF CONTENTS

# LECTURE ONE

## Introduction to the Series

## The Personal Object of the Pastor

### September 29, 1873

AT the request of the authorities of the Boston University, I am here to address students preparing for the Christian ministry in the SCHOOL OF THEOLOGY of this promising and important Institution.

The subject proposed for my consideration is the practical one, which comes under the title of PASTORAL THEOLOGY. I have accepted this invitation with much pleasure, both as a token of the personal confidence and respect which it expresses, and as an occasion to manifest my abiding interest in young men so occupied, and my cordial sympathy with this noble foundation for the promotion of evangelical truth among the influential and intelligent population of this city.

It has been one of the joys of my life to mingle in the mutual offices of edification, encouragement, and sympathy with "all those who love our Lord Jesus Christ in sincerity."[1] Under the providence of our common heavenly Guide, my own ministry has been pursued in that old Church of the Reformation, one of the fruits and progeny of which is the active and wide-spreading Christian body to which this school of theology belongs. But I gratefully acknowledge "one body"[2]

---

[1] Ephesians 6:24.
[2] Romans 12:4,5; 1 Corinthians 10:17; 12:12,13; Ephesians 4:4; Colossians 3:15.

among all the disciples of our gracious redeeming Lord; and in this assembly I feel myself in reality as much at home as if I had as openly taken the arm of Wesley, as I have truly desired to imbibe the spirit and to exercise the power of Whitefield, in the great purpose and warfare on earth, in which both were so equally and truly engaged.

The direct object and purpose of my present personal effort among the young servants of Christ, to whom I now address myself, is not to bring any scheme of mere dogmatic theology, or to make any attempt at learned or critical course of theoretic instruction. I have been invited to give them, on the general subject proposed to me, some of the results of my own observation and experience in a long and active life in the Christian ministry; as a familiar testimony of facts, rather than as a preconceived theory of opinion: and this I shall desire and endeavor to do.

More than fifty-three years of active ministry, forty-four of which have been passed in the two great cities of Philadelphia and New York, have certainly given me large opportunities for such observation and experience in this most important field of social and religious life. And much ought to have been gathered from such a field which might be made useful to younger brethren in this comprehensive and all-important work.

A life so active and occupied has given little opportunity for those collateral and incidental pursuits in literary and scientific attainment which are the delight of the educated mind, and the peculiar claim and distinction of the age in which we live. The successful professional man becomes habitually too exclusively professional to allow himself the relaxation of much diversion, or to permit the distinction of eminence in any walks of mental research beyond the limits of his own selected path. Under this constant pressure, I have been compelled to say, in the language of the great apostle, "This one thing I do."[3] But I have found a life so organized and occupied a most happy sequestration of time and thought, of energy and means of

---

[3] Philippians 3:13.

influence, when thus completely given to ministering to my fellow-men, "both publicly and from house to house, the unsearchable riches of Christ."[4]

Some of the results and acquisitions of such a life I have been requested to give to you, my younger brethren in Christ. This I shall endeavor to do in a manner perfectly simple and conversational; and with some illustrations in facts, which must be considered unavoidable, and will be regarded perhaps as not altogether undesirable, in the line of thought and suggestion which I have been requested here to exhibit and impress.

In carrying out this effort, I shall assume an entire unity of general sentiment and purpose with me among those to whom I particularly speak. As an earlier traveler in the road of our united selection, I come back to aid, if I may, those who are following me, by telling them something of the path as I have found it; some of the things which I have seen and learned upon the road; and some of the joys and trials, the mistakes and the means of safety and success, which I have met; as prepared for others who travel it with a sincere, upright, and earnest spirit.

Fifty-four years have gone since I left this old and much-loved Boston, my father's home, as a home for me. But age and years have in no degree lessened the home love of a "Boston boy;" and to other boys of another generation I come back to speak of the interesting subjects proposed to me here.

To give some aspect of form to utterances which would be likely to become too desultory and heterogeneous without some scheme proposed, I shall proceed to speak of PASTORAL DUTY, rather than PASTORAL THEOLOGY: of the *concrete* of *action*, rather than of the *abstract* of *principle* and *power*. In accomplishing this design, I shall cast the whole subject into a consideration of the CHRISTIAN PASTOR, in HIS OBJECT, HIS QUALIFICATIONS, HIS INSTRUMENTS, HIS AGENCIES, HIS POWER, AND HIS ATTAINMENTS..

In introducing the general subject, I must remark that the Christian pastor is the Christian preacher, occupied in the

---

[4] Compare Acts 20:20; Ephesians 3:8.

private, relative personality and application of his work. The two separate titles present aspects which are reciprocally complemental and adjuvant to each other.

But they involve tasks, to say the least, so separate and discriminate in their details, that it is by no means actually frequent that the same person becomes equally successful in both departments. Indeed, each of these departments of duty so completely demands the whole man, that the success in the one exercise is frequently rather the alternate of success in the other; and yet they are but two parts of a living organism, properly conjoined, and improperly separated. They ought never to be, and they can not safely be, torn asunder. The same man can be both, and can be better in each when they are properly united than when purposely giving his whole mind and attention exclusively or mainly to either apart.

To place these two offices of the Christian ministry in comparison for mutual illustration, we may say the Christian preacher is the public official teacher of divinely revealed objective truth. The Christian pastor is the private acknowledged minister of the same truth, in its personal application and subjective individual experience.

Distinctively, the one exercise of this twofold office requires especially an intellect divinely enlightened, and the peculiar ability publicly to expound these great things divinely revealed, as ministering salvation to the soul of man. The other needs especially an affectionate and sanctified heart, and the power of an active, discerning sympathy, ready to meet the varied conditions of ignorant, suffering, or advancing man.

The special gift for the one is extending knowledge of the great and glorious revelations of the Gospel. The gift needed for the other is a deepening personal experience and observation of their practical worth. To the one, a clear intelligence and comprehension of these divine declarations of truth, in their general aspect, are essential. For the other, a discriminate consciousness of the proper persons, and the appropriate conditions of human life, to which these heavenly instructions are to be applied, is needed.

Together they present a vast field for human attainments, and for relative, personal influence upon man. Age and study, prayer and faith, love and earnestness, and persevering fidelity, are indispensable to them both. But in the Christian ministry, as in the medical profession, younger men, with whatever talent, must practice mainly by their knowledge of the efforts of others, as described in books or imparted in lectures; while older and more mature agents habitually prescribe upon the results of their own observation and individual experience.

Thus is it with the ministers of the Gospel of the Lord Jesus Christ. Youth presses on, in an opening, expanding road, under the imparted guidance of those who have successfully preceded. Age even more firmly rests for its duties in the future upon its own retrospection of the way already traveled. The incidents, facts, and principles of action, which have been already demonstrated in the light of the past, become the advisers and guides for the obligations of the future.

It is scarcely possible to separate these two offices of the Christian ministry in our personal consideration of them. But we must not forget that the Christian pastor is the generic office and character. The Christian preacher is this pastor in the exercise of a single gift, in the fulfillment of a single office, in this one great and comprehensive purpose and work, appointed and established by the Lord of all.

In proceeding to consider the special relations of the pastoral work, we can not magnify the influence, the usefulness, or the dignity of this divinely established office among men. The Almighty Savior, the great Head of the Church of God, is himself the Chief Shepherd; and his whole redeemed Church are his flock—the sheep of his pasture. He feeds them. He leads them forth. He goes before them. He is their guide, their example, their watchman, and their provider.

And he says to those whom he calls to unite with him and to follow him in this gracious work, "As my Father hath sent

me, even so have I sent you." "Feed my sheep. Feed my lambs."
"Lo, I am with you alway, even unto the end of the world."[5]

Such is a general view of the office and work of a Christian
pastor. In the impressive language of the Episcopal Liturgy, they
are "called to be messengers, watchmen, stewards of the Lord; to
teach, to premonish, to feed, to provide for the Lord's family; to
seek for Christ's sheep that are dispersed abroad, and for his
children, who are in the midst of this evil world, that they may
be saved through Christ forever."

In proceeding to discuss the specific and relative character
of this office, in the details of its operation, I can not enter upon
any particular discussion of preaching, as a portion of its proper
fulfillment. My appropriate purpose leads me to consider with
you the private, personal ministrations of the Gospel of our
Lord as the special field for the pastor's office.

To the importance and special efficacy, under the blessing
of God, of this ministration for Jesus from house to house, "in
season and out of season,"[6] the combined experience and
wisdom of the Church of Christ will testify in perfect harmony.
Dr. [Isaac] Watts has said that the man who has the happy talent
for parlor preaching may often be made the instrument of more
good in a few hours than others can do without it in many years.

Fifty years ago a very distinguished layman of the
Methodist Church, who had himself been long a local
preacher—a man of education and large influence—said to me:
"They are not the great preachers in our Church who are the
most useful to us, but the faithful, earnest pastors. Our revivals
come more from prayer and private exhortation than from
public preaching."

About the same time a very influential layman in the city of
Washington said to me of one of the Episcopal clergymen of
that city, by no means a great or eloquent preacher, "Mr.
H_____ is an angel in a sickroom. His visits are to me like
heavenly visits."

---

[5] John 20:21; 21:15-17; Matthew 20:28.
[6] 2 Timothy 4:2.

My whole personal experience and observation in the long period since passed have fully confirmed the truth of such estimates.

I knew a very fine preacher in the Episcopal Church who was wholly unsuited in his tastes and absent habits for the work of a pastor. His ministry became the subject of conversation, and the question was asked, "Why is not Dr. S_____ more practically useful? The work does not seem to prosper with him." The answer made was, "He loses the whole of his Sabbath influence in the week. He is like a farmer who had surrounded his land with finely turned posts, but neglected to put up his panels of fence, and wondered why the cattle strayed in upon his ground. Well-turned posts will not keep cattle out, nor secure the prosperity of the field. You must put up your panels of fence. Your weekly pastor work is your fence. Nothing else will guard the Savior's work, keep out opposing influence, or secure a harvest for the honor of the Lord."

But we will proceed to consider our subject more distinctly in the order which we have proposed: What is the personal OBJECT of the pastor in the Church of Christ? What has he been sent into the world to do? The attempt to discuss such a theme as is here proposed in a single address like this, with any practical efficacy, will prove, in the necessity of the case, an extremely superficial and fragmentary work. But still I propose to you the question: *For what is this Christian pastor intended, in the personality of his office, by the Lord who has sent him forth and commissioned him for his own service on the earth?*

I answer you: In the very character and structure of his office, he is a divinely appointed messenger, an ambassador, an agent of the Lord Jesus Christ, the everlasting Savior of men, to proclaim and minister his great salvation to the souls of fallen men. He is the authoritative bearer of a divine message—of reconciliation—of pardon—of acceptance with God—of spiritual consolation and strength from a God of infinite love to the homes and hearts of sinful, weary, waiting, suffering men.

He is not merely a Christian gentleman among his fellow-men. He does not go on a voluntary neighborly visit, as a private

Christian friend. He does not speak to others simply as a
sympathizing, intelligent companion, upon his important theme.
He goes as an appointed messenger of Jesus Christ his Lord,
bearing special tidings of salvation in his Master's name, to a
selected household, or to an individual immortal soul. He has
been called and appointed by the Lord himself for this special
work and message now entrusted to him.

Of the particular character and evidences of this call from
God I can not now speak; but I can take no lower ground than
this in the general consideration of this subject in which I am
now engaged. In the Liturgy of the Episcopal Church, the first
question which is proposed to the applicant for ordination to the
ministry is, "Do you trust that you are inwardly moved by the
Holy Ghost to take upon you this office and ministration, to
serve God for the promotion of his glory and the edification of
his people?"

In our present contemplation of the subject, there is to be
considered and conceded a distinct divine call, an inward,
personal motion, to this ministry, for the promotion and
attainment of *a twofold object*, separately relating to the gracious
Savior, by whom, and to the souls of his people for whom, we
are employed and sent. And our mission has this twofold object
always in view: TO GLORIFY THIS EXALTED SAVIOR; and to lead
the *souls of sinful men* gratefully to *receive*, to *accept*, and to *live in*
HIM, and *for* HIM —the HONOR OF JESUS and the SALVATION OF
MEN. And this twofold object of the Christian pastor's life and
mission I ask you to consider in their successive aspects.

The FIRST impelling, attracting purpose in this great work
of your life will be the HONOR of that great redeeming Lord,
whose you are and whom you serve. This will be to you a
distinct, conscious, and defined purpose of your mind and heart.
If the love of Christ really constrain you, this motion of life and
action will be no shadowy imagination—no sanctimonious
pretense; but a consciousness as real, as clear, as practical as any
personal impulse can be, of human friendship, of grateful
recognition, or of social duties, in any of the individual relations
of active life.

Others may discuss as they please, in the cold indifference of intellectual, unbelieving speculation, the reality of the Savior's being and history, the scale of his nature, the questions of his authority. To your practical, individual experience of his love, and earnest consciousness of your own personal love for him, equally distinct, there will be no distracting or retarding questions here.

We "know whom we have believed."[7] To us the word of Jesus is infallible, unchanging truth. His love and active goodness are unsearchable riches of grace. His authority is absolute and entire. "In him dwelleth all the fullness of the Godhead bodily. And we are complete in him. He is the brightness of the Father's glory, and the express image of his person."[8]

We are called to represent him. We go from him. We go for him. We are the bearers of a divine message to be delivered to others, by his authority and for his honor. It is a message of direct salvation from God to man. From God forgiving, to man condemned. This is a message of facts perfected; of a work accomplished; of purposes, invitations, and offers founded upon these facts—the offer of a complete, immediate, everlasting salvation, presented to the faith, to the grateful acceptance, to the affectionate trust of man, in the freest, fullest message: "Whosoever will, let him take of the water of life freely."[9]

This is your message to each, to all to whom you are sent. It is "the old, old story;" yet it is always new, always living, and by God's Holy Spirit always to be made effectual. Wherever we go, we have the same great and gracious work committed to us; and we "are not ashamed of the Gospel of Christ, the power of God unto salvation to every one who believeth."[10] We love to tell this precious story—over, over, and over again—in every house; at every bedside of sickness; in every chamber of sorrow; to every anxious, burdened heart; in the midst of every afflicted

---

[7] 2 Timothy 1:12.
[8] Colossians 2:9,10; Hebrews 1:3.
[9] Revelation 22:17.
[10] Romans 1:16; cf. 2 Timothy 1:8.

household; to every waiting sinner like ourselves, wherever we may find him.

We are never wearied with proclaiming this gracious message from God. We love to repeat this effective intelligence of pardon for the chief of sinners, through the atoning blood of an Almighty Savior. We feel its blessedness; we know its power; we delight to meditate upon it; and we do not fear nor hesitate to proclaim it freely, whether men will hear or whether they will forbear. In this great work, to which the Lord has been pleased to call us, we desire to set him always before us; and to see Jesus only, clothed with glory and honor.[11]

You can not throw yourselves upon the power and truth of the divine message too simply, too constantly, too completely. You need never fear failing in your work by preaching the gracious work of Jesus; or wearying those who hear you by an unwearied clinging to the simple Gospel of a crucified and risen Savior.

Go, tell the world abroad, from house to house, in season and out of season, the things which God hath done, and which God hath revealed. The glory of a divine incarnation—"God manifest in the flesh."[12] The mercy of a personal assumption, by an infinite Savior, of the condition and responsibility of lost and ruined man. The gracious offering in sacrifice of an atoning death—a "propitiation for the sins of the whole world;"[13] the accomplishment of a glorious resurrection; an accepted obedience; a complete and unalterable victory, for guilty but believing man, over condemnation and death. Go, tell with all the earnestness of a loving, grateful heart, of perfect reconciliation from God to man; of real and joyful hope for man in God; of newness and holiness of life—life eternal, a full assurance of hope; all constituting, all meeting in a glorious Christ—a crucified Christ; presenting to every believing soul, complete, perfect, everlasting salvation in him, in whom alone all

---

[11] Hebrews 2:7,9.
[12] 1 Timothy 3:16.
[13] 1 John 2:2.

fullness must dwell forever; and from whose personal fullness believing souls must receive "grace upon grace."[14]

This is your great pastoral work for Jesus on earth. We do not say to you, Go, discuss this great subject; argue about it; show how it can be, or may be, true. Waste your time in no such outside folly. Deliver your message on the authority of the infallible word of God. "Obey your orders," simply, constantly.

A chaplain at Walmer Castle, the official residence of the Duke of Wellington, attempted to apologize for a sermon at which the Duke was unexpectedly present. He was instantly met with the bluff but appropriate reply, "What are your orders, sir? What are your Master's orders?"

You go forth to obey your orders. "In the morning sow thy seed. In the evening withhold not thine hand. For thou knowest not whether shall prosper, either this or that; or whether they shall be both alike good."[15] Wherever you are, tell your precious tidings to some one. The message of that which God has done is the offer of that which man may have. Complete forgiveness in a Savior's death; everlasting cleansing in the power of a Savior's precious blood; unchangeable acceptance with God in a Savior's perfect obedience for man; eternal life, the gracious gift of God in him.

Never be afraid to deliver this message freely. Unlimited in its relation to persons. Unconditional in its offer to individuals. Perfectly candid and free in its approach to every sinful man. Immediate in its full blessing upon the soul believing. To be at once accepted—entire, undivided, indivisible. Bringing perfect, eternal salvation to all who will receive the message, with faith and grateful love toward the one glorious Savior of the lost, perfect and complete in him.

If any object, or revile, or oppose, we simply say, "We are not careful to answer you concerning this matter." "We are doing a great work; we can not come down; wherefore should the work cease, while we leave it and come down to you?"[16]

---

[14] John 1:16.
[15] Ecclesiastes 11:6.
[16] Daniel 3:16; Nehemiah 6:3.

Richard Cecil, a faithful evangelical preacher of the Church of England, received a visit from a gentleman in his study, who came with the proposal to discuss with him the subject of a preceding discourse. Cecil answered him, "My dear friend, I am willing freely to tell you all I know, and to answer any question which I can; but my mind is perfectly settled and satisfied upon the whole of this great subject, and I do not desire any discussion about it."

You do not go out to discuss about the glorious message which you are sent to carry to your fellow-men. You go simply and plainly to teach in your Master's name and with his promised presence and help. You will gain every thing by a simple, honest, affectionate delivering of your message. You will gain nothing by a discussion of its truth or its authority. You will deliver your message. You will earnestly impress its importance. You will beg its grateful acceptance. And you may say, with the servant of Abraham, "Now if you will deal kindly and truly with my Master, tell me; and if not, tell me: that I may turn to the right hand or the left."[17] But deliver your message distinctly, kindly, positively, and without fear. The Lord will bless the faithful witness.

Forty years ago, I was quietly seated in my study, in Philadelphia, when a very respectable gentleman, a stranger to me, introduced himself and said, "I have been round among the churches of this city, anxious to know the way of truth and safety for my own soul. You seem always to speak as if you were perfectly sure, and had no doubt upon the subjects of which you speak. I have been much impressed by your simplicity and constancy of statement, and I have determined to unite with you. I came to lay my case before you, and to confer with you upon the great subject of your teaching." That visit led to his grateful acceptance of the Gospel and of the Savior's love. That man still lives to show the fruits of this precious Gospel in a life of Christian usefulness, protracted to a very advanced age.

---

[17] Genesis 24:49.

Far later in my work, a young man came to me in the city of New York. He was a lieutenant in the United States Navy. He had heard me as a stranger, and he came to my study to present the same general difficulty, and to propose very much the same questions as the one just alluded to. He described the different uncertain and unsatisfying directions which he had received. With great earnestness and emotion, he begged from me a simple guidance in the way of divine truth. I expounded to him, in as clear and short a manner as I could, the full and triumphant scheme of God's salvation as revealed in Jesus, and presented in the one perfect offer of a complete Savior in him, to every believing soul. He listened with intense interest, his countenance glowing with emotion. I said to him, as I closed, "Now, in accepting this glorious system of grace, do you feel yourself a man to *be* saved by any thing that you can do, or as a man *already* saved by that which the Son of God has done for you?"

He answered me, after a little thought, with flowing tears, "I do not see, in your statement of the matter, but I am a man already saved." "Well," said I, "what, then, has a saved man to do?" "I do not see," he replied, "that he has any thing to do but to love, trust, and be happy." "What more can he do?" I said. "That is heaven. That is the whole of such a life forever."

In profuse weeping, he covered his face with his handkerchief and said, "Oh, excuse me, sir. But I have never heard such teaching before." He left me, rejoicing in the freeness and fullness of this precious Gospel of a Savior's grace and love.

I trust I have thus presented to you, with sufficient clearness, a distinct and conscious object in the pastor's work. This is his first object. He goes forth into the field of a Gospel Ministry to proclaim a Savior's fullness, and to honor and glorify this Savior's character and name. This is the first, controlling, commanding object of his life—the honor of Jesus, his glorious Lord. "The sound of his Master's feet is behind him."[18] If Christ shall be magnified in him, this is "all his salvation, and all his

---

[18] 2 Kings 6:32.

desire."[19] And this rewards him for all his toil, whether in life or in death.

I wish you to realize this great principle and fact. We are extremely tempted and prone to lose sight of this great living, practical result of our office and work; and to put some other, but inferior results, which may be the rightful consequences of this one high purpose, before it in place and in degree.

Let me earnestly entreat you, in public and in private, to make all your work, in its highest purpose, its first and its last design, consciously, clearly, constantly, a grateful labor for the Savior's glory; and a determined purpose to count all things but loss for his honor. You are charged with a positive, distinct message from him, to be delivered simply and faithfully to every class of men and to every condition of man. And you will glorify him by "taking of the things which are his, and showing these to men."[20]

This work, in its highest manifestation, is the work and office of the Holy Ghost, and our ministry becomes a ministry of the Holy Ghost, and is in the power and purpose of the Spirit, in the degree in which we unite with him, and under his guidance, in testifying always and only the unspeakable fullness of this glorious, atoning, exalted Savior.

We will pass from this *first* controlling object in a Christian pastor's life, to consider another, which is secondary to this, though in our work indissolubly connected with it. I speak of the effect to be produced upon the souls and the condition of men to whom we are sent. And I shall define this object to be, to bring lost men to a living Almighty Savior, that they may find eternal life in him. We are to persuade their grateful acceptance of his boundless grace, that by the Holy Spirit of God they may be converted unto him; united with him; transformed after his image; made partakers of his fullness; made one with him by the divine power; living upon his work of grace and love for them; and bringing forth the fruits of all goodness to his glory.

---

[19] 2 Samuel 23:5.
[20] Cf. John 16:14.

This is the full restoration of man in character and condition to God; their new creation in Christ Jesus; presenting them perfect, in the fullness of Christ, as an all-sufficient, unchanging Savior; clothed by him with the garments of his salvation; covered with the robe of his righteousness; and reigning in life through him, by him, with him forever; made thus the temples of the Holy Ghost; the restored children of the living God; renewed in holiness, after the image of him who hath created them; and enjoying the restored presence and glory of a reconciling God in his kingdom forever.

Thus you now go forth upon your mission, as the messengers and ministers of the Son of God, to a world of immortal beings, in the various conditions of their human life and of their heavenly privileges.

As we behold the multitudes with whom we meet, however they may indefinitely vary in the aspects and elements of personal character and condition, they present to our view but two distinct classes of persons. Their separation may not be always perfectly discriminated. But it is real and actual. These two classes must never, in themselves, be confounded by us; nor shaded off on either side to a third, and a finally indistinguishable class.

We meet them, and we find them, unaffected by varied knowledge, talent, or personal claims, in the reality of their condition by nature or their condition through grace. They are all either converted or unconverted in their relation to God. They are believing or unbelieving in their relation to the appointed and exalted Savior. They are the temples of the Holy Ghost, who dwelleth in them, or they are without, and are resisting and despising, the Spirit of God. They are the children of God or the children of the Evil One. They are living in Christ and for Christ, or they are living without Christ.

This is a division which, in its elements and distinctions, is vital; and is unalterable but by divine power. We can not close our eyes to its observation, or in our minds refuse its consideration. Our whole ministry to men, in all its details, must be governed by it. To each and to every one of those to whom, in your pastoral work, you are sent, you have a special message to bear from your glorified Lord; differing in its contents and its application, and with a distinctly different purpose in view.

Whether in your public or your private ministry, you must keep always in mind this vast and vital distinction among those to whom you minister. It will regulate your whole work. It will guide you in the language of exhortation, of direction, or of counsel. You can not bless those whom God has not blessed. You can not refuse those whom he has acknowledged and received. You must "take heed that you offend not one of his little ones;"[21] nor "break the bruised reeds nor quench the smoking flax."[22]

With all these, of every class, without reference to their personal, transitory distinctions, your object is one—the restoration of all in peace to God; the salvation of all in the fullness of Christ; the sanctification of all by the power of the Holy Ghost. To them all, we cease not to teach and to preach Jesus Christ the Lord: the living Head, the heavenly Manna, which alone can give life to all who are in the world. But our pastoral application, our particular message of the Word, in its presentation to the varied persons to whom we are sent, will much vary, according to our perception of their special character and condition. To each must be given their special portion in due season.

I am perfectly aware that multitudes, and many whose apparent character I am ready to regard with sincere respect, will not accede to the precision of my statement upon this subject. I know that the minds of many in our time, who claim a special intellectual cultivation, may be disposed to look with much contempt upon assertions and judgments which seem to them so completely fanatical and unreasonable. There is a vast temptation pressing upon those who desire to gratify, or who shrink from offending; or who indulge themselves in imaginations of such advancing light and refinement in the

---

[21] Matthew 18:10.
[22] Matthew 12:20; cf. Isaiah 42:3.

generations of educated men, as shall overturn and banish all such narrow-minded and old-fashioned distinctions of human character as the Word of God has made, to withhold and refuse such precise and positive statements. They would dig down these precipitous cliffs of divine affirmation. They would shade off these antagonistic colors. They would graduate and neutralize these disagreeable demands. They would claim for men externally refined a concession of real and acceptable goodness, which may not belong to those of a coarser nature or a more ignorant condition.

To such imaginations or aspirations of human pride or personal vanity you can yield nothing. You are to speak to all, not according to the wisdom of men, nor in the words which man's wisdom teacheth, but according to the wisdom of God, in words which the Holy Ghost teacheth.[23] The question, 'What is popular?' can never be allowed by us. Our demand is, 'What is true?' You can not forget that God often chooses the weak things of the world to confound those which are mighty. And he will never fail, in his own way, to prosper the fidelity of his servants, or to honor the faithful ministration of his own Word. You may meet with painful rejections of your message, and with great trials of your fidelity. But Jesus will always honor those who truly honor him.[24]

A very upright and much respected merchant in Philadelphia, whose wife was an earnest Christian woman under my ministry, and who was himself often at church, respectful in his deportment there, and personally extremely kind and friendly to me, was suddenly brought to the last hours of his life. At his wife's request, I visited him in his sickness. I pressed upon his attention the Savior's love, and the salvation offered in him to believing man. He completely, coldly, almost angrily, rejected my whole appeal, and finally exclaimed, "Sir, it is impossible. God must have provided some better place than hell for a man of my respectability." And he turned from me, and would hear no more.

---

[23] 1 Corinthians 2:13.
[24] Cf. 1 Samuel 2:30.

I was elsewhere called to the sickroom of an old and respected physician, who had been most civil and agreeable to me in social life. To him I carried the simple message of the Savior's love; the full salvation in a glorified Christ. He instantly turned his back to me, with unconcealable displeasure. "I don't believe a word of it," he almost screamed. "Shall I pray for you?" I said. "You shall never pray by me—I will not hear you," he replied. He threw the bedclothes over his head, and roughly bade me leave his house. And thus he died.

A wealthy planter in my first country parish had been one of my chief supporters and friends. I had often pressed upon him this precious message of the Gospel, but in vain. At midnight, I was sent for to visit him as dying. As I came into his room, he turned to me, with the utmost affection in his manner, but with an expression of real distress, and exclaimed, "Oh, my dear friend, I did not think it would come so soon." I tried to present to him still the pardoning love of Jesus. I knelt by his side and prayed. But his last words, often repeated, were, "Oh, it is too late. I did not think it would come so soon."

We are not always received, but we are not always rejected, in our personal efforts to save the souls of men. A very distinguished man and merchant of Boston, whose name is still here venerated in his posterity, and who was well known to me in our family relations, but whom I had not seen since I was a youth in a counting-house with which he was connected, met me many years ago in the parlor of a hotel at one of the Virginia Springs.

I addressed the few visitors and the families on the Sabbath morning from the words of the Apostle, "Let us go forth to him without the camp, bearing his reproach."[25] This gentleman was a man of unsurpassed aspect and influence and position in society. But he was one of the very men whom I should have expected to be most likely to be offended with the earnestness of my exhortation. During the address he wept in tender emotion, and at the close he came up and took my hands in his and said,

---

[25] Hebrews 13:13.

"What a joy it is to hear you preach such a Gospel. Every word went to my heart." But I was then very young in my work, and he was a man of age and great dignity in life.

Another very distinguished citizen of Boston, a high military officer in the state, was in my church in New York on the Sabbath. Preaching on the importance of simplicity in our message from Jesus, I said as an illustration, "We must surround the walls of Jericho again and again, and blow this trumpet of the Lord, until the walls shall fall." I knew this gentleman well, and I saw him much moved as I was speaking. He came up to me when the service was over, and shaking my hand most earnestly, he said, while shedding tears, "My dear friend, I bless God, the walls of Jericho have fallen flat. What a glorious message this Gospel brings."

Now, my young friends, with this heavenly message you are charged. It belongs to all. It is divinely arranged for all. All have the right to demand it, always and in all places, from those who are sent to preach it. It must be divinely applied to all. It is a simple message from God, whose ambassadors you are. Nothing in it is left to man's invention. When it shall prosper, it is impossible for you to decide. The power is of God alone, by his own accompanying Spirit of Grace and Truth. If you are made the blessed instruments to bring men to Christ, to edify believing men in Christ, to glorify an exalted Lord in their salvation—their walk in newness, holiness, usefulness, beneficence of life—the work is wholly his; and the glory will be his forever.

I pray you never to forget that our success in this work is not from the wisdom, the power, the eloquence, the magnetism, as it has been called, of particular men. It is wholly from the presence and power of the Holy Ghost. In all truly successful men, it is the power of prayer—the power of humble, self-renouncing faith—the power of a close, patient, loving walk with Jesus. This is the power which will always attend the faithful, simple preaching and teaching of a crucified and living Savior—"an historic Christ," as some have profanely called him; of the work which our Lord Jesus Christ has personally done and personally completed; and the fullness of the merit and the power of which dwells in him alone.

We do not preach, as this work of salvation for man, the work which a ruling Savior may do successively, accretively, as the race and the ages go by—the fruits of his divine dominion. But the work which he has once already done, never to be repeated; and the reality of which is increasingly demonstrated by its living power to bless all who believe it, accept it, trust it, rejoice in it, and thankfully look back to it as the one unchanging fountain from which must flow all the streams of that river which makes glad the city of our God.[26]

This, my dear young friends, is your pastoral work, in its exalted OBJECT. It is to glorify the name and the work of Jesus; to lead all men to embrace the fullness of his love and power; to build up all in the unsearchable riches of his grace; to prepare all for the fullness of his glory; to make ready a people prepared for the Lord.

Let me press upon you this threefold object, in your own personal work for Christ. Let this glorifying of Jesus be the Sun which lights your public preaching; the outspreading light which makes clear, attractive, and effectual your private ministrations; the dawn of the morning in the cheerful opening of your life-work for a beloved Savior; the glowing beauty and radiance in the occident of your day completed. Make this, keep it, the calm twilight of your old age, apparently retiring, but only to reappear in a higher glory for a nobler day; when Jesus shall be ALL for you, in a heavenly rest, as he has been your ALL in your earthly work of thankfulness, confidence, holiness, and love.

---

[26] Psalm 46:4.

# LECTURE TWO

## THE QUALIFICATIONS OF THE PASTOR

### September 30, 1873

My young friends, I have attempted, in my previous lecture, to consider with you the twofold OBJECT of a Christian pastor. Every experiment, in which we shall unite, in speaking or in hearing, will deepen your impression and enlarge your conception of the extent and importance of the subjects which we treat, and of the office for which you desire to be prepared. You will find it quite impossible for me, in a few lectures like these, to do more than to offer to you a general guidance and some friendly fraternal suggestions for the anticipation of such a work. With the sincere desire to do this in an edifying and acceptable manner, I shall proceed to our second subject proposed: the necessary QUALIFICATIONS for the work of a pastor so employed.

As you associate with your fellow-men in the duties of a pastor's life, you find them arrayed in two classes, perfectly distinct, and to be accurately discriminated in your personal relations to them. They are UNCONVERTED, perishing in unpardoned guilt, to be brought to Jesus by the Holy Ghost for their soul's life; or they are CONVERTED, living really in Christ, to be edified and instructed in the full knowledge of his salvation, and enjoyment of his favor and presence. And now we ask, 'What are the qualifications which a Christian pastor requires for a work so delicate and so important as this?' 'What is he?' 'What ought he to be?' And I answer, he needs:

I. A real *humanity*, with all the consciousness and sympathies of man. It is quite remarkable how the first apostles for the Lord insist upon this entire humanity of their ministry. In all their work, this must be considered and must not be forgotten; "Stand up," said Peter to the bending centurion; "I myself also am a man."[27] "We are also men of like passions with you," said Paul to the men of Lystra.[28] "Who is Paul? who is Apollos? but ministers, even as the Lord gave to every man."[29] "We have this treasure in earthen vessels; the excellency of the power is of God."[30] It is made the definition of a true minister of Christ, and the reason of his selection, that "he is compassed about with infirmities, that he may have compassion on the ignorant, and on them that are out of the way."[31] This is the divine pleasure that by the mouth of sinful men this great message should be ministered to a world that is to be saved.

This humanity of the ministry makes an important element of its power and of its usefulness. When its trials beset us; when its responsibilities overwhelm us; when its apparent failures disappoint us; and our hearts are sad and anxious in this survey, we must look at the fruits of this experience. We must not forget that of our glorious Lord it is said, "Because the children were partakers of flesh and blood, he also himself likewise took part of the same."[32]

The whole work and provisions of the Gospel are addressed to the weakness, the necessities, and the experience of our humanity. Thus all is plain. The Savior's love for sinners led him to partake of their infirmities. And in our ministering the knowledge of this love to our fellow-men, all our own humanity is demanded. We must enter into the sorrows which we would

---

[27] Acts 10:26.
[28] Acts 14:15.
[29] 1 Corinthians 3:5.
[30] 2 Corinthians 4:7.
[31] Hebrews 5:2.
[32] Hebrews 2:14.

assuage and heal. We must taste of the infirmities which we are called to alleviate and sustain.

This is by no means a light aspect of our work, or of the demands which it will make upon us. It often taxes our highest powers; demands our utmost patience and skill; exhausts all that we can know or do; employs our deepest consciousness of personal sinfulness; and compels us to renew the remembrance of the guilt and danger which we have ourselves tasted and felt. The conscious bitterness of our own unbelief; the sorrows of our perverse alienation from God, and rebellion against him, are made the strange instruments of comfort to others. And we are constantly teaching and encouraging the weak, the weary, and the desponding, from the sad recollection of our own wanderings and falls, as earthen and broken vessels. How sweetly the Lord intimates this thought to Peter: "I have prayed for thee, that thy faith fail not. When thou art converted, strengthen thy brethren."[33]

We never get deeper convictions of personal sin than in our attempts to console and guide others in their hours of darkness and guilt. We are never more truly or effectually made the "sons of consolation"[34] to them than when we are secretly weeping, in the bitterness of our own souls, over past personal transgressions, of which they have no consciousness or knowledge; "comforting others by the consolations wherewith we are comforted of God."[35] How Paul recalled the bitter cruelty of his own career, when he was pouring out his mortal life for the glory of his Lord and the defense and guidance of his people. How often in the history of the Church the vilest of men, like Augustine and John Newton, have been called to the widest, deepest, and most experimental consolation and instruction of the people of God.

You have thus to go out upon your life-work as pastors in the flock of the Great Shepherd, with a constant reminding, and with a deepening humiliation under this growing consciousness, that in the very experience of your humanity you are prepared to be the comforters of those who find no other friend. You need

---

[33] Luke 22:31,32.
[34] Cf. Acts 4:36
[35] 2 Corinthians 1:4.

not describe the errors and follies of your life past. But if you have tasted the bitterness of death; if you have been with Jonah in the deep, with the weeds of death wrapped around your head; if you have been consciously in your spiritual state once dead, and then made alive again by the power of the Holy Ghost, the very sorrows and sins of your human history have been a gracious preparation, under the amazing goodness of God, for your deeper and wider ability to comprehend and to meet the sorrows which others bear, and the sins with which they are laden. This ability is one effective element in the usefulness of your pastoral life. You know and feel and understand all the difficulties, trials, weaknesses, and sins which others meet in striving to gain their foothold firm on the rock of God's salvation.

II. The Christian pastor must be a CONVERTED man. His important work can not be accomplished by the wisdom and power of man in the mere force of his own intellect, or by his own knowledge of the amenities and advantages of a mere virtuous life. He goes out to gather and to feed the flock which Jesus has purchased by his own blood. To suppose an unconverted man divinely called to this important work, is to suppose a wolf entrusted with the sheep by an infallible Shepherd—an evil against which the Savior most earnestly warns. "Ravening wolves in sheep's clothing,"[36] he calls them. That a man unconverted should be called in that state to minister the Gospel of the Son of God by the Lord himself must be esteemed an impossible thing. The experience of a converted man is essential to the pastoral work. The whole work depends upon personal qualifications. The guidance which is to be given calls for a personal knowledge. On no other basis can the pastor succeed. A man may be converted after he has entered upon the ministry. But he can not be a true minister of Christ until he is converted. To confer with an awakened, anxious mind, or with a sick and suffering soul, in the mere formalisms of an outward Christianity, is a fearful assumption. The man who is alive to God will know how to point out the way to others. He is at home in this

---

[36] Matthew 7:15.

great crisis of immortal life. He speaks the things which he knows. And the Spirit of God guides him and follows him with his new creating power.

Sometimes the directions which are required will he very peculiar in appearance. I will illustrate this by an incident which gave me much encouragement in my early ministry.

At an inquiry meeting which I held in Philadelphia, where more than fifty persons were assembled, I marked a young man, well dressed, but with a flashy air, which awakened some suspicion of his sincerity, and I left him until the last, when we were left alone in the room. "For what purpose did you come here?" I said. "To find salvation for my soul," he replied. "Are you really sincere in this?" I said. "Perfectly sincere," was his reply. It was late in the evening; I said, "Will you meet me in my study tomorrow evening at eight o'clock?" "I will," he said. At the appointed hour I was waiting, and he came. He gave me the history of a wild and self-indulgent life; of a faithful Christian wife, slighted in a refusal of her expostulations, and distressed by his wanderings. I opened to him the way of salvation, and urged him to embrace it. But he declined to take any religious stand, though apparently sincere in his anxiety and desire—withheld apparently by the opposition of his own pride. After an adequate conversation and prayer, I said to him, "If you are really sincere in the wish you express, are you ready to go home and say to your wife, 'I have lived a sinful life long enough; I am determined from this hour to give up this life of sin, and live for Christ alone;' and kneel with her, and pray for the Lord's blessing and acceptance?" He was silent for a while, and then replied, "No, I can not." "Then," said I, "I have nothing more to say." And I took up the book which I had been reading. Three successive times I said to him again, "Are you ready now to do this?" At last I heard him draw a heavy sigh, and saw his eyes glistening with tears. "Will you go now?" I said. "I will," he replied, and rushed by me and departed. I had never seen the young man before.

The next evening was one of my weekly lectures. As I stood in the desk, I saw this young man come in, with a young woman leaning on his arm, whom I had often seen there alone weeping: a woman of a sorrowful spirit. They came forward to the front bench before me, and knelt together on the floor. When the service was over, I approached them and said, "Is this your wife?" He answered, "Yes." I turned to her and said, "This young man promised me last night that he would go home to you, and say that he was determined to live for Christ, and kneel and pray with you. Did he do it?" "He did," said she. "And how do you feel tonight?" I said to him. "Oh, sir, I am the happiest man in the city of Philadelphia." That young man lived to adorn his Christian stand in a useful life; and after a lingering consumption was called to die. The last time I was at his bedside, I said, "William, do you remember the evening you were in my study?" "Remember it!" said he, raising his wasted hands and arms to his utmost reach, "Oh, I shall never forget it through all eternity. It was the birthday of my soul."

This interesting illustration is by no means singular. You will often find a truly converted ministry for Christ thus rewarded. But to be useful ambassadors for him, you must really understand what conversion is, and ask and expect the blessing from his gift. To be a converting minister, your pastor's life must be a converted ministry.

Let me present you another illustration. Some years ago I was sent for to visit some strangers at a hotel in New York. They were a widow lady, whom I had known in South Carolina, and her son, a young man, who was very ill. I learned from her that a clergyman whom I knew had visited him, but had no conversation with him. From this gentleman I received the statement that he found the young man so much excited and talking so strangely that it was impossible to hold any conversation with him, and he therefore only said a prayer at his side and left him.

I was introduced to the chamber of the young man. Upon a cot in the middle of the room lay a singularly interesting youth, perhaps twenty years of age. Beside him sat a female cousin, a young lady about his own age. His mother said, "Julian, this is Dr. Tyng." He fixed his earnest black eyes upon me, and stretched forth both of his hands to me and said, in the most beseeching tones, "Dear Dr. Tyng, my mother has often told me about you. I am very sick, and must die. My mother has always told me I must be converted. I must be *converted*. I am not converted. Oh, how can I be converted?" These earnest expressions he repeated several times. I told him simply of the love and fullness of Jesus; of the open way of salvation, in loving and trusting him; that real love and faith toward Jesus was the work of the Holy Spirit, and was conversion. His countenance was the very impression of anxiety and earnestness. I prayed with him for the Savior's own teaching and acceptance, and left him. The next day I called again. He was lying as I had seen him before, apparently in repose. His countenance was the emblem of perfect peace. He awoke and welcomed me with the sweetest, loving smile, and said, "Oh, dear Dr. Tyng, I understand it now. Jesus has forgiven me all. And I truly love him. And the love of Jesus is conversion. How sweet and precious it is. Dear mother, I am converted. Am I not converted?"

This was the peaceful, heavenly state of his mind for some days; and in this he departed, happy and at rest. His young relative, who was with him, was converted by the gracious influence of this occasion, and became a very valuable servant of the Lord. His brother, who was also there, a young physician, despised it all, and avowed himself to me an Atheist.

I present you these illustrations of the way in which the Lord is pleased to honor a ministry which strives to honor him. This whole point of a truly converted ministry I wish to impress upon you. The pastoral ministry requires all the sympathy of a converted man. The whole efficacy of its work is dependent on this. In vain will you attempt to deal with awakened, convicted, inquiring, anxious minds without the experience and tenderness which really is in Christ. The ministry demands the example of a converted man. One great purpose in the human ministry is in the pattern which its truly sanctified character presents; so that it can say, "Be ye followers of me, even as I am of Christ."[37] Others will follow us, if we truly follow Jesus. The ministry demands the motives of a converted man. Its trials in a faithful pastor's life are peculiar, unending in time. Our difficulties and our warfare change, but they never end till life itself must end. All shams and pretenses will die under this pressure. Nothing but the love of the converted heart for Jesus, and for the souls of men for whom he died, will keep the heart up to the work. Every motive will perish, but a real, living faith in a Savior, *known* and *loved* and *chosen*, as our only portion and our only subject.

III. The Christian pastor must be a man CALLED OF GOD. I can not go with you into a didactic exposition of a divine call to the ministry in these simple, practical lectures.[38] It is the infallible testimony of the Word of God, "No man taketh this honor unto himself, but he that is called of God."[39] And it must be to you a most important and impressive subject for personal examination and thought. "How shall they preach except they be sent?"[40]

Such a call to the ministry is the subject of personal, individual experience. Paul says, "It pleased God to reveal his Son in me, that I might preach him among the heathen."[41] In all its aspects, this divine call is a transaction between the soul and its Redeemer. It gains its interpretation from the sacred Scriptures of his inspiration, and the man himself must feel it and know it.

It can be nothing less than a deep and solemn conviction and constraint of personal obligation. "Woe is me, if I preach not the Gospel."[42] You can never safely look upon the ministry as a profession, the entrance to which is spontaneous and subject to choice. It is a dispensation, an *"Oikonomia,"* a law of

---

[37] 1 Corinthians 4:16; 11:1; Philippians 3:17.
[38] On this subject C.H. Spurgeon's valuable *Lectures to my Students* contains an excellent lecture on the call to the ministry. In it he quotes from a letter of John Newton that has very wise counsel on this subject.
[39] Hebrews 5:4.
[40] Romans 10:15.
[41] Galatians 1:16.
[42] 1 Corinthians 9:16.

the household of God; rising above the mere acknowledgment of duty, to an experience of the constraining love of Christ; to an appreciation of the infinite value of the Gospel, which we have been taught by his own Spirit and power, and the joy and hope of which we have truly and clearly received.

This sense of obligation to Jesus, to the souls of perishing men, is absolute and constraining. His precious Gospel has given life to our souls. This is the life by which we really live. We know its power; we feel its truth; we comprehend its worth; we must preach it to our fellow-men. Its unsearchable riches of grace we must and will proclaim whatever it may cost; whatever it may bring of earthly care or of earthly trial.

The pastoral ministry can be effective only with such a call from God. What I mean, I will take the liberty to illustrate by a short statement of my own experience in connection with it; not as a rule for others, but as partly the source of my own conviction.

After being graduated at Harvard University, I was for two years in a large East India counting-house on India Wharf, in Boston. I lived a formally moral life, though with no real knowledge of a Savior, nor having any pastoral ministry over me which could instruct me in his truth. My earthly engagements and prospects, in the engagements which I had made, were considered by my friends very brilliant and secure. I was wholly devoted to the demands and prosperity of my worldly plans, and I had no want beyond them.

I awoke in the early morning of the 19th of July, 1819, with a voice which seemed to sound in my ear, with the solemn appeal, "What a wasteful life you are leading!" I answered in my silent conscience and heart, "I will live so no longer." I immediately arose from my bed, and, without dressing, knelt upon the floor, and gave myself in my poor way to a Lord whom I did not know, but by whose voice I fully believed I was called. I went down as usual to my business. But my whole mind and purposes and plans were changed. The world of wealth had passed out of my view. A load of sin pressed upon my heart. But I knew no outward instructor who could comprehend my wants or guide my way. Thus I groped for days, without one earthly comforter.

Nearly opposite the head of this street in which we are now assembled, adjoining the Tremont House, you may see a small quadrant spot of grass enclosed. It is all that remains of a large and beautiful yard, which was then the residence of Mr. Adam Babcock, one of the leading men of Boston in that day. The whole residue of the property has been incorporated in the site of the hotel. In that courtyard dwelt a retired nurse, long in the family, in rooms prepared for her. She was a venerated Christian woman, who was familiarly called by all the branches of the family Aunt Minott. Some of my young female connections told her the strange news that "Stephen Tyng was out of his head in thinking and talking about religion." The old lady sent a message desiring to see me. She was a Methodist. The family, like myself, had always been in the congregation of Trinity Church. Her Christian home was "Bromfield Lane Methodist Chapel." That old lady was the first Christian friend I found who knew a Savior's love, understood a Savior's Gospel, and could enter into my heart, having received this Gospel neither by man nor from man. With her I could talk of Jesus, and not be deemed insane.

A single month passed before, under the pressure and guidance of that Spirit by whom I had been called, I left all the business of earth and gave myself simply and wholly to my Savior's work. I was considered insane by many, in a world which looked only to its own things. I have no doubt that many of my friends really lamented over me as insane. But whether I was beside myself, it was to God.[43] I gave up all the prospect of wealth before me, and determined to preach my Savior's Gospel. My dear father, with whom I lived, replied to my proposal of this change: "Are you crazy? You are throwing away the most brilliant prospects of any young man in Boston" I answered: "I was never more sane in my life, sir. I can not help it. I know that I am called to preach the Gospel. I know that there is some place between here and the Rocky Mountains for me to preach my Savior's love. I am going until I find it." The venerated man was overwhelmed. "Well," said he, "you will spoil a first-rate

---

[43] Cf. 2 Corinthians 5:13.

merchant to make a very poor parson." "It may be so, sir; but I must go." He was spared to me for ten years after that interview, to value most highly my poor attempts, to encourage with the utmost affection my efforts in the Savior's cause, and to gain part of his consolation in death from my grateful ministry. This was "my manner of entering in."[44]

I sincerely, deeply felt that I was called to preach this precious Gospel. More than fifty-four years have since passed by, and I can not say that I have ever had one doubt of the Gospel which I preach, or of the fact that I have been called of God to preach it.

With great self-abasement, but with entire confidence, I can truly adopt the language of St. Paul: "When it pleased God, who separated me from my mother's womb, and called me by his grace to reveal his Son in me, that I might preach HIM, immediately I conferred not with flesh and blood."[45]

I really do not speak of this in vain boasting, but humbly to illustrate what I understand and mean when I say to be an effective Christian pastor you must be "called of God." You must be taught the way by a heavenly power, and willingly go where his Providence shall send you, spending and being spent, publicly and from house to house, that you may bring sinners to the knowledge of a Savior's love, and build up his saints in their most holy faith; by his grace preventing you, going before you, giving you the good-will, and working with you in carrying out that will to good effect.

Thus qualified by the sympathies of a loving manhood—by the new creating power of the Holy Ghost truly converted—by a conscious, satisfying call from Christ your Lord to your important work—you may become thus far prepared to be effective, faithful Christian pastors for the flock of Christ.

IV. The Christian pastor must be a man of A SYMPATHIZING NATURE AND HABIT. It is impossible to imagine a hard man—a censorious, fault-finding man—a man fretful,

---

[44] 1 Thessalonians 1:9.
[45] Galatians 1:15,16.

easily annoyed—a man taking gloomy views of men and things, of divine providence and guidance—to be an effective, useful pastor. How simply and tenderly the apostle describes the office, as he had felt it and had endeavored to execute it! "We were gentle among you, even as a nurse cherisheth her children. Being affectionately desirous of you, we were willing to have imparted unto you, not the Gospel of God only, but also our own souls, because ye were dear unto us." "We exhorted, comforted, charged every one of you, as a father doth his children."[46]

This is a temper which does not become fatigued or worried with the unceasing calls upon a pastor's sympathy, consideration, and effort. I think there is no employment on earth which involves the same amount and variety of occupation and care. There is no question or interest of domestic, social, or personal life which does not come before a faithful pastor's mind and notice, with some particular and pressing demand in the prosecution of his appointed work. He must care for all, plan for all, bear with all, and strive to "become all things to all men, that by all means he may save some."[47]

To meet all these demands effectively, he must maintain the constant life and power of religion in his own heart; the life of God in his own soul.[48] He must grow in an increasing sense of his own personal need. He will meet with many trials of temptation and of temper, which will show him what manner of man he is, whether easily provoked, self-indulgent, and unyielding, or whether he is really becoming forbearing, patient, disinterested, and gentle.

He must grow in an enlarging perception of the fullness and blessedness of a Savior's love. Nothing can sustain him amid all the worrying trials of a pastor's life but a deeper work of this twofold growth of true piety: the stock of the one bearing *a ripening humility,* and the branches of the other blooming and waving with a higher, brighter, more *abiding and precious hope.*

---

[46] 1 Thessalonians 2:7,8,11.
[47] 1 Corinthians 9:22.
[48] See the book *The Life of God in the Soul of Man* by Henry Scougal (Sprinkle Publications, VA), which was used to bring George Whitefield to Christ.

All acceptable ministry rests upon this twofold experience. We can not effectively, privately teach beyond the line of our own personal attainments and real sympathy of feeling. When we get beyond that which we have felt and seen, I will by no means say that all our teaching is false and a sham, because it may be perfectly sincere in its motive and desire. But it is a mere lecture from second-hand information. We are telling the things which we have heard, and of which we really know little. Our own deepening experience of the need and power of the Gospel is essential to our advancing usefulness. We become the more qualified to be the guides, helpers, and teachers of others as we suffer and gain the more for ourselves.

This twofold power of our ministry, wherever we may be in our pastoral work, depends upon the reality of this growing sympathy. We sometimes receive very severe lessons of peculiar ministerial experience, to test and to increase our forbearance and our pastoral strength and usefulness. Among the many rules for a useful and happy life in the ministry which my venerable relative and teacher, Bishop Griswold,[49] gave me in my studies with him, one was, "Never vindicate yourself." I do not know that I have ever violated this rule in a single personal instance. Every pastor will meet with some trials which will demand and test it.

In my first permanent charge, in the southern part of Maryland, there was one man of commanding influence and wealth, from whom a large proportion of my support had been derived. Circumstances entirely beyond my control led to his personal alienation from me, and excessive persecution of me. He publicly defamed me, by charging me with lying. I took no personal notice of the charge. When one neighbor after another among the planters of a wide country parish came to me to ask the truth of his statements, I made but one reply: "Go, ask Mr. C. himself." "But he has already said so. What is the use of going

---

[49] Alexander Viets Griswold (1766-1843) After being elected bishop in 1811, Griswold underwent a conversion experience. His preaching and piety became markedly evangelical. A tremendous spiritual awakening occurred throughout his diocese. Church membership increased approximately tenfold between 1790 and 1840. He was a leader of the evangelical movement within the Protestant Episcopal Church.

to him?" was the answer. "Well, if I should contradict, I should simply throw the charge of falsehood upon him. What should I gain by that?" Five years of that persecution passed, in which he yielded nothing. It cost me much of comfort and peace. I removed at that time to Philadelphia. There, some months after, I received a letter from my successor, saying, "Mr. C. is very ill, and can not live. He begs me to write to you for him, and ask your forgiveness before he dies. He is filled with bitter remorse. He says he has never ceased to respect you during the whole period of his persecution of you, and that he can not die in peace without receiving your forgiveness." On the outside of the letter was a memorandum of the hour of his death. You can judge the comfort which I received from the remembrance that I had never avenged myself, even by words, nor been suffered to be cast down by the distress of the persecution.

Thus in our own suffering we are made to understand the sympathy of personal endurance. But, beyond this, there will be an active sympathy demanded from you in every variety of human woe. No class or station of those to whom you minister will be found released from burdens or sorrow. The troubles may often be imaginary in their source; but the sorrow and the suffering are always real. You must not only appear to sympathize, but your heart must really go out, "weeping with those who weep, and rejoicing with those who do rejoice."[50]

The widow and the fatherless, the poor and the neglected, the downcast and the forgotten, the sick and the sorrowing; those for whom no other man will care, and whom no other man will help; the convicted, the persecuted, and the sinning, are all the portion of your inheritance, and you must sympathize with all.

If you have no heart for all this line of outward demand upon your time, your thought, and your affections, the pastor's office is not your gift. What a perfect description you have of what a successful pastor really enjoys, and of what a faithful pastor really does, in the 29th chapter of Job. What can more perfectly describe the unfailing sympathy of which I am

---

[50] Romans 12:15.

speaking? "I delivered the poor that cried, and the fatherless, and him that had none to help him. The blessing of him that was ready to perish came upon me. I caused the widow's heart to sing for joy. I was a father to the poor, and the cause which I knew not I searched out."[51] The apostle Paul brings all the illustrations of this fine testimony upon an evangelical basis of description and experience when he says, "Who is weak, and I am not weak? who is offended, and I burn not? I will very gladly spend and be spent for you, though the more abundantly I love you the less I be loved." "I seek not yours, but you."[52]

I would urge you, my young friends, watch over, cultivate this spirit of coterminous sympathy with the sufferings and the sorrows of all whom the Lord shall commit to your charge, and so illustrate the mind and fulfill the will of Christ, your Great Example and Lord.

V. Besides all these, and through them all, the true CHRISTIAN PASTOR must be A PATIENT MAN; ENDURING, IN ALL LONGSUFFERING AND PATIENCE, THE IGNORANCE AND THE INFIRMITIES OF OTHERS. Perhaps I have seen parish difficulties arise as often from the impatience of ministers, as from the discontent or the hostility of the people. A sensitive and weary student is often very little able to contend with the petty annoyances of local life.

I knew an unhealable breach made between a very distinguished minister and a contiguous neighbor, which ended in the removal of the former, from the killing of the minister's chicken by the layman's son. "Behold, how great a matter a little fire kindleth."[53]

A clergyman of some celebrity called on me with this statement: "I am in great difficulty in my parish; all the women have turned against me." "Well," said. I, "then you must certainly go. No man can stand in a useful ministry against the hostility of all the women. But what has been the cause of so

[51] Job 29:12,13,16.
[52] 2 Corinthians 11:29; 12:14,15.
[53] James 3:5.

much difficulty?" He replied: "The organist in my church is a young lady belonging to one of the best families in the parish. Her mother is the leader of the choir. The choir is a voluntary one, under their direction. They all serve without pay. One Sunday, when I was going from the vestry-room into the church, I heard the organist playing a very light and improper tune, as a voluntary. I rose from my private prayer, and, turning to the organist, I said, 'Stop that music—I will not have *Annie Laurie* played in my church.' They were all so offended that none of them came in the afternoon; and since that all the families have taken it up, and there is so much difficulty that I know not what to do." What could I say to him under the circumstances, but "the sooner you remove from there, the better both for you and the church?"

A man who could so foolishly and coarsely give offense could not have discretion enough to avoid offense in the future. All mere circumstantial advice would have been lost on such a man. He removed to another state, and has since departed.

An impatient, hasty man can do nothing as a pastor. He may be esteemed, perhaps, as a very fine preacher, and be acceptable in that office while an unexamining popularity attends him. But such a man can do nothing as a pastor. He is too self-seeking to be sympathizing; too explosive to be patient. He will find endless quarrels with vestries, trustees, and committees—with women and families—until his peace has gone, his reputation has been destroyed, his presence is unsought, and his whole heart is worn out. The best excuse you will ever hear of him is the equivocal defense, "The poor man is too sensitive to be happy or useful."

The trials of patience, of self-possession, for a faithful pastor are sometimes very great. He is often, as Jude says, "pulling men out of the fire."[54] As Paul describes it, "Fighting with beasts at Ephesus."[55] But even in such a crisis, a faithful, patient, self-possessed pastor will always succeed at last. Let me give you an illustration of such a trial.

---

[54] Jude verse 23.
[55] 1 Corinthians 15:32.

A very fashionable and wealthy family was professedly under my care in Philadelphia, but living wholly in the world and for the world. By the blessing of God, the Word reached the hearts of the mother and the eldest daughter, a young woman. They were converted. Their whole manner of life was changed. The ballroom was renounced; the prayer-meeting was adopted. The life of fashion gave way to a life of faith. The father was a merchant, of wealth and great social ambition; he had delighted much in the beauty and style of his wife and daughter. His indignation was intensely aroused by their change of character and life; his anger knew no bounds. He watched the gates of the church, to prevent their attendance by authority and force. When we received them to their public Christian profession, we were obliged to admit them through the back window of the basement in the church.

These painful circumstances required all of a pastor's wisdom to visit, to counsel, and to aid them. One night, at a very late hour, as I was retiring to my rest, and my family was all withdrawn, a sudden ring of my door-bell summoned me to answer the appeal. It was a servant of this lady, who said, "Mrs. B. wishes you to come immediately to her house." She could give me no further account. I prepared myself to go, telling my wife whither I was going. I supposed that I should meet some scene of violence, and I knew not what might be the result to me.

I was admitted to the house by the same servant who came for me. A single lamp lighted the hall. All seemed dark beyond. I was led into the front parlor, where, seated upon a sofa behind the door, I saw this man, with his face covered with his handkerchief, and his wife sitting at his side. She simply said, "Mr. B. thought he would like to see you, and I took the liberty to send." With that he exclaimed in broken accents, "I wish to know whether there can be salvation for a wretch like me." "Surely," said I. "But what has led you to ask such a question of me?" "This angel woman," said he. "I thought you the blackest of human beings. You had broken up the peace of my house. You had alienated my wife and daughter from me. I determined to kill you. I have watched at the corner of your street several nights to shoot you, but you did not come by. I have beaten this angle in my anger. I have dragged her through these rooms by the hair of her head; but she has never spoken one harsh word to me. She has prayed for me; she has been more loving to me than ever before; and I can stand it no longer. Can there be salvation for a wretch like me?" His wife tried in vain to moderate the language of his appeal.

This man united with his wife and daughter in their Christian profession, and became to me a firm and useful friend. By God's blessing, patience had its perfect work; and his house seemed to them all perfect and entire, wanting nothing.

In the same revival in our church, another very similar man, not quite so violent, treated his wife, under like circumstances, with intense ridicule. He called her, at his own table and before her children, "My little Jesus Christ." Of him I heard nothing better than continued reproach. So far as I knew, he maintained his bitter infidelity to the end. But I ceased not to uphold his persecuted wife with encouragement and consolation to the utmost of my power.

A Christian pastor's patience must endure through all such scenes and trials. His sympathy must never fail. His watchful earnestness must never cease. Unwearied at all times, night and day, in season and out of season, bearing all things with unfailing love. With a spirit and habit so maintained, he may be permitted to reach large blessings from his toil. Without this, prophecies must fail, tongues must cease, knowledge must vanish away.

The wise son of Sirach says: "My son, if thou come to serve the Lord, prepare thy soul for temptation."[56] Without all patience and longsuffering, as well as sympathy, knowledge, and labor, you will never be able to accomplish or to endure the demands of a Christian pastor's work.

VI. To all these most important qualifications, I shall add REFINED AND GENTLE MANNERS AND HABITS. The Christian pastor must be a gentleman, in the moral derivation of that title.

---

[56] This quotation is taken from the Apocryphal book Ecclesiasticus 2:1, written by the son of Sirach about 200 years before Christ. Although not part of the Holy Scriptures, like other writings of men, it contains many helpful words.

True Christianity in its practical manifestation is *refined humanity*, in its emotions, conceptions, desires, as well as in its habits. Too really right to be assuming; too consciously dignified to be pretentious or foppish; too clear and exalted in spirit to be careless or dirty or offensive in personal habits. Innately conscious of the proprieties of personal relations. Not "despising dominions, nor speaking evil of dignities."[57] Perhaps there is often more real pride in vulgar indifference to propriety of manners, to places, and persons, than there is in the cultivation of the most fastidious regard to little relative proprieties of civilized life.

The Christian pastor is admitted, by the respect and courtesy of civilized society, to families in every station as an equal friend. He may associate with the best bred and the most cultivated families with whom he meets, receiving their cheerful and happy welcome. And he is wholly unfitted for his place and duty if he disgusts by his boorish habits; offends by his coarse and undignified familiarities; or discards the controlling amenities and refinements of cultivated society.

"I tread on the pride of Plato," said Diogenes, as he walked across the Persian carpet which covered the floor of the philosopher. "Yes, and with more pride than Plato," answered the philosopher to the Cynic.

Perhaps you may smile, if I give you a few little illustrations of unrefined habits, in some things, which have come under my notice. But John Wesley did not think it beneath his high sphere of duty to give particular instructions to his preachers, even how they should leave their beds and chambers in the morning, when they had enjoyed the hospitality of friends.

Within my knowledge, a minister who was lodged in the best chamber of a Christian lady, who had welcomed him with much pleasure to her house, painfully disgusted her when she found in the morning that he had taken the nice embroidered covering from her bureau to wipe his face and hands, though a rack of clean napkins was openly in the chamber.

---

[57] Jude verse 8.

A minister once officiating for me wiped his nose and face in the midst of the public worship with the sleeve of a clean linen surplice, instead of his own handkerchief, to the great abhorrence of many who saw him.

A minister in commencing his public prayer in a highly furnished pulpit, in my sight, took out of his mouth a large piece of tobacco, and laid it down upon the marble slab which finished the desk, and when his prayer was finished deliberately put it into his mouth again.

I could narrate many such illustrations of coarse and disgusting habits and acts. But I have no doubt that many such violations of propriety in personal deportment have been known to you all. I would have you realize that these are not trifling or mere artificial things, peculiar to the habits and tastes of a single class of society. Refined and gentle habits are even more demanded in officiating among the poor than among the rich. There is a sense of propriety among the least educated and the most limited in earthly means, which shrinks just as instinctively from coarseness and roughness, from vulgar ways and rude habits, and which is impressed just as really by the manners and deportment of well-bred and careful persons, as among the richest families with whom you will associate.

Affected contempt for all these external things, as they are sometimes called, may become the disciples of a down-treading infidelity. But such indifference is wholly repulsive to the refining purposes, principles, and habits of true Christianity.

A well-educated young preacher of my acquaintance visited, at her request, an aged Christian woman, whose circumstances in outward life were very limited. After his departure, her spontaneous exclamation was, "Dear bless you. How sweet he is. Why, he is all sunshine." The kind and graceful manners of the young minister did her good, like a medicine. I was once with a gentleman in the church of the celebrated Dr. Bedell,[58] of Philadelphia, who was extremely impressed by his personal aspect, apart from his ability as a preacher. He said to me afterward, "Dr. Bedell is the finest specimen of the manners of a clergyman, of pulpit manners, that I have ever seen." Perhaps there was never a minister who was a more perfect example of a real, tender, pure, loving, unpretending, Christian pastor than Dr. Bedell. He was a perfect St. John, in that special imitation of his divine Lord; associating with all as an equal, and making all to feel as wholly equal to him in his society. I pray you; do not accustom yourselves to think these elements of no importance in your pastoral life.

I must conclude this review of selected qualifications for a useful pastor's life and work. The value of a faithful cultivation of all these you will hereafter fully estimate. But they must be acquired at the beginning. The certainty of an acceptable and successful ministry will grow out from them.

With a conscience and heart rightly directed; with a mind enlightened and taught by the Spirit of God; with a scheme of motives sanctified and elevated; with habits of personal religion fixed and real; with a communion with your exalted Savior cultivated and established; with a sincere love for the souls whom he hath redeemed, implanted and cherished within you; with your consciousness of human infirmities awakening a brother's interest in all around you; with a real conversion, which has brought your whole soul and life into living unity with Christ your Lord; with an undoubted call by the Holy Ghost, which has separated you to the work to which your Lord has appointed you; with a tender sympathy, an unwearied patience, a generous and friendly spirit, and genial and refined manners in the sight of all among whom you dwell—your morning will be full of promise; your whole career will be happiness continued—owned by God, honored by men; your retrospect will be gratitude and

---

[58] Gregory Townsend Bedell (1793-1834) served in the Protestant Episcopal Church in Philadelphia, PA until his health broke down.

peace. The sun which has shined sweetly through the day will sink in a repose honored and beloved, and always remembered with delight when evening comes.

But all this depends, not on genius—not on unusual brilliancy of talent—but on a simple, persevering, earnest fidelity to Christ your Lord, which works contentedly, thankfully, happily, in every place and in every relation, because it works every where *for him*. These are the qualifications which fade not, fail not, disappoint not, discourage not. With these, you will all be made vessels of honor, meet for the Master's use, because you are proved to be every where vessels of the Holy Ghost, by whom Christ is formed in you the hope of glory, and through whose power Jesus dwelleth in you, and you in him.

# LECTURE THREE

## THE INSTRUMENTS OF THE PASTOR

### October 1, 1873

My young friends, in the two previous lectures I have dwelt upon the OBJECT and the QUALIFICATIONS of the Christian pastor in the fulfillment of his important office and work.

I propose now to speak of the INSTRUMENTS which he is to employ in the practical fulfillment of this work. Suppose his object to be clearly defined and understood; his qualifications to be ample and appropriate; himself ready to undertake his responsible office and duty in the variety of practical, personal demands which it must necessarily make upon him. The question immediately arises, as a most pressing one, 'How shall he be made able to fulfill the wide and varied demands which are to be made upon his thought and skill?' There are manifestly two separate provisions needed by him—*appropriate instruments* for his appointed purpose, and *skill* to use them successfully.

There is scarcely a more helpless person than a youthful pastor in his first personal connection with the souls for whom he is to watch, and whom he has been called to feed. To preach the sacred Word in public, with a few prepared sermons, is easy and pleasant, and scarce involves any anxiety. To deal alone with individuals—awakened, anxious, suffering souls—demands a wisdom and discernment which will rarely be found in the opening of a young man's work in this important ministry. It is to stand, in conscious weakness and ignorance, to meet all the wants of an immortal being in a crisis which we but little understand. It may well alarm and cast down the timorous and halting mind. And yet, if we go forward in the spirit of conscious sincerity, leaning upon our appropriate and promised help from the gracious Savior who has sent us, we rarely fail; we are soon enlarged, instructed, and enabled to go forward with success.

I well remember my first experience of this searching demand. At nineteen years of age I had just entered upon my regular candidateship and study at Bristol, Rhode Island. I was even then a constant preacher. Coming out of church one Sunday evening after a very solemn service by the venerable Bishop Griswold, during which he broke entirely down, and was conducted out of church before the service was regularly concluded, I saw a company of persons gathered round a large square pew in the middle aisle. As I joined them, I saw a young woman under deep distress of mind, and I was asked to speak to her. I will not attempt to repeat the follies of my attempt. Perhaps I did not appear to others so foolish as I seemed to myself. But if I had been called to command and steer a ship, I should hardly have felt more incompetent. And yet that very mortification was very instructive to me for my then coming work—it made a part of my preparation for teaching many.

But I can say most truly to you now, that no demand in life can be more serious and searching as an employment than this spiritual dealing with awakened souls. And this is one most important department of a pastor's life. The Holy Spirit alone can give the ability accurately and usefully to deal with it. But HE will instruct and bless the feeblest effort of sincerity in the Lord's service. And while you go forward in your Master's work with a true and faithful heart—whether as messengers to call, as watchmen to protect, or as pastors to feed and provide for the children of God—there will be a divine power always attending you, applying the word which you speak in conscious feebleness, with living energy, and giving you increasing encouragement every day.

I will illustrate this fact by the next experience of mine to the mortifying one already stated. That very Sunday night was the last of the Bishop's preaching for more than eight weeks. There was no other one besides me to be his substitute, and to maintain the public and private worship and the meetings of the church. And this was the commencement of a very remarkable revival of religion, which, under that head, I shall hereafter describe. Within a few days I was called to visit a poor sailor-boy who was ill in a consumption. He had been a wild, wandering youth from his childhood. When I first saw him in this bed of poverty and distress, he seemed to me as spiritually ignorant as the Greenlanders among whom, in his whaling voyages, he had been. I questioned in my own mind whether he was competent to be taught the precious truths of the Gospel. With his widowed mother he lived alone, utterly destitute and deserted, in a small, wretched cottage in the outskirts of the town.

But wonderful was the lesson which God had graciously prepared for me at that bedside of poverty and distress. I daily read to him the precious Word of God. I told him of the love of Jesus to the lost and the wretched. I prayed by his bedside every day. My whole heart went out to him in loving sympathy and earnestness. Divine light from the Savior's countenance soon burst upon him and upon me with heavenly brightness. This poor, outcast boy, emaciated, with his bones literally wearing through his skin, was filled with the Holy Ghost, with all joy and peace in believing. The gracious Spirit, in teaching him, was every day teaching me yet more and more abundantly.

The poor youth partially recovered, and in the opening spring was able to be out. He was visited and encouraged by others. His case became well known in the church. Some months after, I was conducting one of the Conference meetings of the church. In the dim light, in the extreme part of the hall, a man arose and asked permission to give an account of the Lord's dealing with him. He told his story with a deep, hollow voice, but in language of singular simplicity and beauty. Every heart was moved; every eye wept in grateful sympathy. It was my poor sailor-boy, whom I had thought too ignorant to be taught. But he had become, under the blessing of God, my teacher. Soon after this he departed, with the clearest hope in Jesus, and with an intense, absorbing love for his divine Redeemer.

The history and experience of that sailor-boy have been to me a perennial comfort and joy in my constant remembrance of him. So far as I know, he was the first fruits of my boyish ministry, and he has been a divinely appointed guide to me, in my memory of him, through all my years succeeding. I have never since doubted the power or the fullness of that exalted Savior to raise the most sunken, or to transform to an angel of light the most darkened and ignorant of the lost children of sorrow and sin. The torch of divinely imparted hope and confidence, which was lighted at the side of that poor boy's bed, has never fallen from my hand, in a ministry since so largely demanded and tried.

What, then, are the INSTRUMENTS by which such a ministry is to be carried out? I do not now speak of the POWER, by which alone, with any instruments employed, we can obtain a blessing. But what are the instruments in the use of which we may justly expect that blessing—the accredited instruments of a pastor's work?

I. I answer, first, the WORD OF GOD *thoroughly believed.* I emphasize this word. We may truly apply the divine testimony to this ease, "Whatsoever is not of faith, is sin."[59] As pastors, we are sent to teach this heavenly truth, the Word of the living God. It is our duty to feed the souls committed to us with the bread of God, here provided, for giving life to the souls of men. We go with this inspired Word, in our hands, in our memories, in our hearts. We do not, we can not go beyond this Word of the Lord, less or more. We receive it, as Paul received, as "given to us, by the inspiration of God."[60] Every word of it is good, as the Lord hath appointed it, and as it was "spoken by men, who were moved by the Holy Ghost."[61] It is, to our implicit and

---

[59] Romans 14:23.
[60] 2 Timothy 3:16.
[61] 2 Peter 1:21.

entire faith, just as clearly and truly a revelation from God, turning upon the poles of everlasting truth, as if the Book we hold were the single copy in the world, given from God, expressly to us, and we had received it, as Moses, in the burning mount of Arabia, or as John, from the opened heaven, in the glowing solitude of Patmos.

Whatever thorough or searching study we are able to give, of manuscripts and versions, of collateral testimonies and subsequent objections, will undoubtedly be a part of our preparation for our work. But all that work of preparing and examining, necessary as it is, must be entirely separate from this actual preaching in the parlor, or teaching by the bedside, and in personal conversation with the ignorant and inquiring.

The pulpit, even, is no place for the discussion of the authority of a message, or for any apologetic defense of the Word of salvation which we are sent to proclaim. We are ambassadors for Christ, not to argue the authority of our commission, nor to heed the reproaches or the objections of those to whom we are sent on this errand of the Lord. Even there, there is no worth, nor will there be any advantage in this time-serving concession.

I was in company once with a well-educated gentleman in one of the Southern States, who had heard, from a minister of some repute, a long sermon, addressed to a large congregation of country people, on the evidences of Christianity. He acutely remarked, in reference to the defects of the sermon, "One of the strongest evidences of the divine origin of the Gospel to me is that it stands, and has stood, through ages of such inadequate preaching." To his view, the preacher was called to preach the Gospel, and not to defend the authority with which it came.

But if we should concede that this outside work at any time becomes the pulpit, it has no place in this pastoral work. In that, we go with the clear, calm resting of our minds and hearts upon the certainty and fullness of this Word of God. We readily impart all the information we have; we freely tell all we know; we aid, as far as we are able, all the infirmities we meet; but our one instrument is the absolute truth of the Gospel. Our message is the love, the death, the glory of Jesus. Our authority is the everlasting Word of God. Our employment is instruction, not discussion. Our power is in the great truth which we are sent to preach, and in the attending guidance of the Spirit, who blesses and applies it. The more simply you tell the fullness of your Master's love, far the better is your work for all, and especially for the educated and the reflecting portion of your hearers.

But when we come to this work of private ministration, this daily pastor work, in proportion to our faith and our reality, in the use of the Word of God is our success. All doubts and questions must be left behind. We are to go upon a direct, divine, personal mission, with minds thoroughly established in the truth we teach, imparting it in the simplest and clearest way to all to whom we are sent, as adapted to their particular case and need. And you will always find that the children of God delight in the language of their Father's Word and their Father's home.

In my pastoral rounds in a Southern country parish, I visited a widow lady whose afflictions had been very great. Her only daughter, a lovely young companion in her solitude, I had buried but a few months before. She had since lived entirely alone. I found her in bed, with a large Bible spread out before her in which she was reading. I expressed my pleasure in finding her so employed. "My precious Bible" she said; "what should I have done this long and lonely winter without my Bible? I have had none to talk with but that dear Savior who speaks to me in this precious Book." This is an illustration of the way in which Jesus speaks in his own Word, and gives us new encouragement to rest upon it.

Go out thus in your pastor work, with the Word of God, thoroughly believed, steadfastly, gratefully adopted—never yielded, never allowed to be questioned or doubted in your mind. The more steadfast and absolute you are in this, the more abundantly and really will your work prosper, and your souls be blessed.

II. A second, most important instrument in your pastor work will be A PERSONAL KNOWLEDGE OF THE GOSPEL CLEARLY UNDERSTOOD AND CLEARLY EXPRESSED. I have lately seen the phrase "The plan of salvation" ridiculed, as a form of expression, by a very popular public speaker. There is, notwithstanding, a very clear, consistent, and well-defined plan of salvation in the Word of God. Let us not forget that salvation for man must be wholly an external work—by an agency separate from man. No man can save himself. If he be not lost, ruined, and in despair, there can be no real desire for salvation, nor any effective sense of its need. The soul can not find salvation in its own duties or attainments, nor in forms or sacraments or religious usages and observances. To direct a man to his own strength or works for salvation is but telling him to pull himself out of the ditch, into which he has fallen, by the hair of his own head. Yet in this skeptical and self-confident age there is a fearful amount of this retroverting and introverting direction suggested to men.

But we can not go forth upon any scheme of this kind. The work which we need, and to which we must direct, is not by human might or power, but by the Spirit of the living God. The edifying and nourishing truth, the truth which gives life to the perishing soul, is always and only the glorious and finished work of the Lord Jesus Christ, embraced by a living faith in the mind, the heart, the conscience of man. The soul can not feed upon any other than this living manna, this bread of everlasting life. And the wisdom, the power, the discrimination of the pastoral ministry are here displayed.

The family of a very sick lady in my flock, during a temporary absence of mine, sent for a neighboring minister to visit her within a few hours of her death. She was beyond the reach of conversation, and he did not attempt that. But he proceeded to administer the sacrament of the Lord's Supper to her, in this almost insensible condition, probably while she was wholly unconscious of his design. Her daughters told me that she died with the bread in her mouth, and with the wine dripping over her cheeks, with her lips closed against it.

This was his exercise of a pastor's work in such an extremity. It seemed to me almost a blasphemous perversion. Many similar illustrations of the varied perversions of a Gospel ministry might be given. The skepticism of one will rest in duties and virtues of man. The formalism of another will propose outward rites and ceremonies. The true Christian pastor, in private as in public, preaches and teaches of the glorious finished work of Jesus, and of Jesus only. The precious evangelical message which he carries is the glad tidings of the glorious fullness of a Savior's work, the completeness of a Savior's offering, and the merit of a Savior's righteousness, to be received, accepted, and rejoiced in by grateful, believing man. And the power of the Holy Spirit of God will attend this faithful ministration of the Gospel, and open and apply the message, to the salvation and the joyful experience of the believing soul.

This is our message and our instrument. By the bedside of sickness, in the house of affliction, in all the anxious trials to which we minister, we are to tell, in the simplest terms, of that one gracious, all-sufficient Redeemer, by whose death the sinner has been ransomed; in whose precious blood the soul is to be washed and cleansed; by whose perfect righteousness the believer is to be justified; and by whose infinite power the pardoned soul is to be carried on through grace to glory.

We are to go every where and to every one with this message of life eternal in the only-begotten Son of God. This is God's merciful provision, and this is our effectual instrument. He has given to us to understand and to value the message, to believe in its authority, to feel its power, and to be willing to suffer its reproach. In the faithful fulfillment of this divinely appointed work we are always caused, by the blessing of God, to triumph in Christ Jesus our Lord. And we suffer nothing to divert us, or to repel us, from the utterance of this one grand message—a full, free, and everlasting salvation, for every soul of man to whom the message comes, and by whom it is received, in the perfect, unchangeable fullness of a personal, exalted, glorious Savior.

For this persevering simplicity of teaching we are sometimes reproached and perhaps ridiculed. In a meeting of ministers in the vicinity of New York, one gave an account of a Sunday which he had passed in that city. In the morning he had been to hear Dr. T___, he said. Another asked, "What did he preach about?" "Oh, he is always about the same thing—forever exalting and glorifying Christ." An aged minister present exclaimed, "Did any man ever give a nobler tribute to another than you have thus given to him?" You may be reproached by the unbelieving, the self-righteous, and the skeptical. But God your Savior will honor your work and yourselves for your unchanging fidelity to him.

I was requested to visit a very fashionable and giddy lady, sick at a hotel in New York, by a faithful friend of hers. The lady herself was a Universalist by her own assertion. I found her surrounded by a number of gay and gaudy women. Novels and newspapers were strewed over her table and bed; and the whole aspect of the place was trifling and vain in the extreme. One of her friends said, "She is very sick, do not alarm her." I declined all interference, and sitting by the side of her bed, I told her freely of the Savior's work and fullness, and of her own necessity for such a Savior for her ruined soul. A solemn silence filled the room while I was speaking. All seemed to be controlled by a divine power. I knelt by her bed and prayed for her and for all. Whether I should be rejected or received, I did not consider. The event proved that the Lord had sent me, and that it was his work in which I was engaged. That visit, and that Gospel which she had never before heard, for she confessed herself to have lived without a church or Sabbath, were made the divine instrument for her salvation.

My next visit found her very differently employed. Her only companion was the Christian friend who had asked me to visit her, and who was a member of the Baptist Church; and she herself held in her hand a Testament, which she was apparently reading. She had opened it at the eighth chapter of the Epistle to the Romans. She said, "I have not been able to get beyond this first verse, 'No condemnation to them who are in Christ Jesus.' Oh, what a precious testimony! What a truth that is!"

I saw much of this woman for years after this. She became one of the most intelligent and truth-loving Christians to whom I have ministered. She has long since been admitted to the glory of that Savior's presence whom she was thus enabled to accept and love.

I would press upon you the importance of these two great instruments in a pastor's work: your BIBLE, accepted by yourself without a doubt of its divine authority and appointment, and employed in your own experience as unquestionable and sanctifying truth; and the precious SCHEME of free and full salvation in the Gospel contained therein, and maintained, employed, presented by you every where to every soul, with constant earnestness; with perfect freedom, and with entire assurance.

In this system of faithful, prayerful labor, the work of the Lord will prosper in your personal private efforts to save the souls committed to you, and to edify the people of God in the love, the faith, the holiness which his Word prescribes. I do not now speak of these two instruments as elements of your own spiritual growth, and thereby secondary instruments of your pastoral usefulness; I speak of them as direct, positive instruments of active influence upon others; and to be put into use and operation by you— simply, boldly, constantly—in all your pastoral ministrations, as messengers of Christ, and as the educators and guides of a peculiar people, for his service and glory.

III. A third and most effective instrument in your pastoral work is HABITUAL PRAYER, for and with all to whom the Lord is pleased to send you. This will include your own unceasing exercise of this precious privilege in your own private hours and relations, as God's appointed instrument for your own personal edification. No class of Christian men so much needs the constant influence and efficacy of personal private prayer as the ministers of Christ. They are not only compassed about with the common infirmities of humanity, but they have very peculiar temptations of their own. They need constantly to cultivate personal and relative affections, which are heavily tried in all the circumstances of their professional life. They need a constantly guarded reverence for God and the things of God. The old proverb, "The nearer the church, the farther from God," is by no means a mere profane imagination.

There is much in the handling of sacred things to make them common and forgotten. There grows a familiarity which inclines very rapidly to indifference and contempt. In every aspect of his inward experience, the minister of Jesus needs watchfulness and prayer without ceasing, to keep him in constant remembrance of the wants of his own soul, and of the holiness of the Being whom he professes to serve. There is much in the freedom of mutual clerical intercourse, where the natural unbending of a common restraint among mutually confiding brethren creates an unusual levity, which up to a certain point is a helpful refreshment, but which also leads to a natural excess, far from edifying, and possibly very injurious. And to keep ourselves in our most holy faith, and to edify each other in the love of God, there is needed for us a constant "praying in the Holy Ghost."[62]

We have thus impressed upon us the necessity of the cultivation of a habit of personal, private prayer, for our own individual growth, in the communion of the Spirit, and in the mind and image of Christ our Lord. The immediate secondary influence of such a habit acts directly and effectively upon the character of our pastoral life. The

---

[62] Jude verse 20.

shining countenance which true prayer, however secret in
its exercises, brings from the presence and fellowship of
our glorified Savior, can never be hidden from those with
whom we dwell and upon whom we act. The man of private, personal prayer is known far more widely than he
wists, and is discovered far more frequently than he
supposes.

But I am speaking here of relative, intercessory prayer:
habitual prayer for all to whom we are sent as the ministers
of Christ and the pastors of his flock. How precious is this
permission for relative intercession. How much we
habitually gain from the prayers of the Lord's people, the
children of our Father in Heaven, for us.

I was once welcomed in a visit to a very godly and
spiritually minded child under my ministry, confined with
consumption, in her last sickness (she died at sixteen years
of age), with this affectionate utterance: "Oh, my precious
pastor," so she always called me, " I have had a most lovely
night of prayer for you. I have spent my waking hours—for
you know I can sleep but little—in telling our dear Savior
the blessings I wanted him to bestow upon you and your
dear son." That son was my eldest, whom the Lord was
pleased to take from a very useful ministry many years ago.
"Perhaps I ought not to say a whole night; but more than
half the night I have been praying for you, and I know that
Jesus will hear me. You know Jesus always hears our
prayers. My precious pastor, this is what I think: first, God
the Father loved me and chose me to be his child; second,
God the Son loved me, and came to save me, because I was
his child; third, God the Holy Spirit loved me, and came to
call me, and tell me that I was his child. Is that right, my
precious pastor?" How precious to us are the prayers of
such real and loving children of God.

Thus should we constantly, earnestly spread the
names, the conditions, the wants of those whom God has
committed to our ministry before him. "We share the
blessings they obtain." Their various trials, their dangers,

their homes and households, should be constantly, frequently presented to a prayer-hearing Savior. We should preface every distinct pastoral effort and visitation with particular prayer. We can not really fulfill or endure the cares and burdens and wants of our condition and office in any other way. There will be constantly questions, applications, cases, difficulties, wholly belonging to other people in their immediate relation, laid upon us, in the adjusting of which God alone can direct or enlighten us. We bear thus obligations, demands, entirely beyond our wisdom or our power to meet, and which most frequently we can not communicate to any human ears. We have no recourse, no instrument of relief, but the mercy-seat of a reconciled and ruling God. We go upon many a personal mission in which we are at our wits' end. Our gracious Leader alone can open and make clear our way. Our people will never know on earth what hours of care, anxiety, distress, and earnest intercession we have watched for them. Scarcely exaggerated is Paul's expression, "My little children, for whom I travail in birth again, until Christ be formed in you."[63]

But I wish to speak also of direct and vocal prayer in our actual visits as pastors of the flock. There may be many obstacles to this habit, especially in large cities. But if it be possible, no pastoral visit should be made without prayer. Let it not be too officiously or professionally interposed, but naturally flowing from our whole character and the natural influence of the visit which we have made. Far more often than we are ready to believe, Jesus meets us with a special blessing in this affectionate, intercessory prayer.

A young man in my congregation, who had finished his college course in New York, and had passed two years in France for a scientific education, came home an avowed infidel. He sunk into a wasting and fatal sickness after his return. His mother, a sincere Christian, begged me to visit

---

[63] Galatians 4:19.

him. I was received by him personally with respect and gratitude. But he would yield to no instruction from me. He was unwilling to listen to me at all upon the great subject for which I came. It became to me a very painful and depressing mission. But I persevered in my visits. He tried in vain to prevent my kneeling at his side, and to excuse himself from attending to me. I might say unceasing prayer was made to God for him by many Christian relations. Weeks went by, apparently in vain. But God who heareth prayer was working quite beyond us. After one visit, in which, as usual, I had earnestly presented to him the fullness and the love of Christ, and besought him to accept the Savior in his heart with love and thankfulness, I knelt as usual by his couch in prayer. He turned his back to me and his face to the wall. In the earnestness of my prayer, I laid my hand upon him, and pressed him to me. He afterward told his mother with delight, that in the midst of that prayer, the tenderness of my manner and the thought of my faithfulness to him first really awakened and impressed him, and the love of Jesus filled his heart with new and wonderful feeling. When I saw him again, his face was animated and elevated in a very peculiar degree. I needed but a glance to see that he was really a new creature. Henceforth the Scriptures were his delight. He would have them read to him continually. It became a joy indeed to minister to him. He sank quietly away in a few days after. His mother, listening to his dying whisper, heard him repeating the twenty-third Psalm. The last words she caught were, "I pass through the valley and shadow of death. Thou art with me—guide me, lead me."

What a gift to the ministry is the conversion of such a youth! What a privilege to a pastor is the open door of prayer! What an instrument does prayer become in a pastor's work when he is enabled to pray with the spirit and with the understanding also![64] Learn to cultivate this habit

---

[64] 1 Corinthians 14:15.

and employment. Keep the edge of prayer bright and sharp, appropriate, intelligent, instructive, Scriptural, and spiritual.

Thus, with a mind established in the Word of God, thoroughly believed, accepted in the infallible truth of its inspiration from God; enjoying the discriminate and experimental knowledge of the Gospel, clearly understood; living in personal communion with Jesus as your known and beloved Savior; moving and acting in the spirit and exercise of prayer unceasing—the pastor's life will be to you no life of trial or weariness, but a life of friendship, influence, usefulness, and unspeakable joy.

IV. A fourth most important instrument in a pastor's work is manifest, simple FIDELITY TO JESUS. I mean an undisputed life that is really one with him, and a living epistle for him, known and read of all men.[65] You will meet with a very quick perception, among the people over whom you watch, whether you are real and true in your personal Christian walk, or whether you are only professional agents and shams. The pastor's usefulness depends almost entirely upon the confidence of the people with whom he is called to associate. Real, affectionate trust, meeting him, welcoming him, aiding him, is more than half of his ability to do good to them.

What you need at all times is that which the Apostle calls "simplicity, godly sincerity."[66] I call it here a simple fidelity to Jesus. It is being in the world, as he was in the world. Having his cause, his authority, and his glory manifestly the one commanding object of your life. And of this I now speak, as an instrument for your personal usefulness as pastors of his flock.

There is sometimes an assumed separation, an apparent, studied, professional holiness, in the aspect and manners of a minister, which repels and disgusts. It comes in sight, with a kind of barking warning, "Stand by thyself,

[65] 2 Corinthians 3:2.
[66] 2 Corinthians 1:12.

come not near to me; I am holier than thou." There is also sometimes a cold, professional air, which gives the immediate impression of a relative loftiness, a want of sympathy with the weakness and ignorance of others. There is sometimes a levity of manner in the opposite extreme, which appears completely inconsistent with the serious, commanding interests and themes which have been committed to the Christian pastor.

I refer to all these now simply in their instrumental character; the inevitable effect which they have in their operation upon a pastor's influence, acceptance, and usefulness among the people to whom he has been sent. The one of these series will create unceasing obstructions in a pastor's way. They shut against him a multitude of outward doors; and they more thoroughly exclude him from that heart-confidence without which all his efforts and purposes will be vain.

But in a life and walk consentient, manifesting the kindness of heart, the wisdom of discernment, and the watchfulness of deportment which distinguished the mind of Christ and the character of his apostles, the Christian pastor finds a welcome in every habitation. Every door is opened to him. Entire confidence is reposed in him. He becomes the chosen adviser, the tender father, the unchanging friend, the desired and beloved companion of every family. All hearts are entwined around him. As a father among his children, he moves among a united flock, the guardian, the guide, the friend of all.

Many such men have I seen, and traced from youth to age in the ministry of Christ. Their fidelity to him was open and undeniable. They were men of prayer, men of experience, men of holiness, men of high and controlling motives. They knew and they taught his Word. They carried with them his example and his influence. They were honored with a peaceful and fruitful ministry. The ear that heard them, blessed them. The eye that saw them, bore witness to them. Their power was undeniable, and every where acknowledged. It was not the influence of popularity, as public performers, nor the acknowledgment of superior intellect or of literary attainment. It was the commanding power of undeniable holiness, disinterestedness, tenderness, pureness, and love. They were universally believed to be right; their judgments stood like a rock; their words, their instructions, were received as unquestionable and undisputed truth.

You can not magnify the importance of such an instrument for the Christian ministry; you can not enhance its actual attainment of happiness, of usefulness, of reverence, of reciprocated love. They attend it as a halo of light, brightening every home of life, and crowning the memory with almost an apotheosis of grateful transmission.

There is no other relationship in life so surely happy or so abundantly remunerative. "My more than father—my more than father," exclaimed one of the noblest of women and wives whom I have ever known, as, weeping with joy and thankfulness, she threw her arms around her pastor's neck, to whom she said she owed every thing that a father-less, helpless child could owe to a Christian pastor's care and love. "My precious pastor, my ever constant friend, what would this world have been to me without you," said a widow, to whom in affliction and solitude God had been pleased to send what she called her highest gift in that faithful, loving friend.

Such tributes are not special, nor unusual. They follow the ministry of every man who comes from Christ, lives with Christ, walks as Christ, every where carries Christ, speaks like Christ, and in all his ministry, in public and in private, preaches not himself, but Jesus Christ his Lord.[67]

In reference to this one sure instrument of usefulness in your pastoral work, I must say to you, "Covet earnestly the best gifts, but here I show unto you the more excellent way."[68] Be faithful to your Lord, and he will make all others

---

[67] 2 Corinthians 4:5.
[68] 1 Corinthians 12:31.

faithful to you. With this undoubting confidence in the Word of God, this clear understanding of the glorious Gospel which it contains, this life of personal, intercessory prayer, this walk of earnest and undisputed fidelity to Jesus, you will be truly clad with the whole armor of God, as the "great heart," the defender and guide of his chosen family, in their pilgrimage through grace to glory.

V. This might seem to complete an adequate view of necessary instruments for the pastor's work. But there still remain some smaller but very important means of usefulness in a pastor's life, which come in connection with these, and exercise a relative influence of great value. Among these I would refer to a CONTENTED HABIT and TEMPER and UTTERANCE.

The importance of this you can hardly magnify. I have seen the best education and intellectual gifts completely overwhelmed in their exercise by a complaining and dissatisfied spirit.

The fundamental theory of our ministry is that we are consecrated a living sacrifice to Christ, and are no longer our own, or at our own disposal. Our whole lives belong to Jesus. Wherever we are placed, we are divinely placed, under a Providence which is over us as the ministers of Christ, with a peculiar, paternal care. The Lord's gracious utterance to his prophet may be applied with equal truth to us, "Thou shalt go to all that I shall send thee, and whatsoever I command thee thou shalt speak. Be not afraid; I am with thee to deliver thee, saith the Lord."[69]

Our immediate location may be by ecclesiastical appointment or congregational election. But with either it is to be for us, with a clear perception that the voice of the Lord is heard, and the will of the Lord is to be done. The spirit of contentment and thankfulness becomes the response of our heart to the word of the Lord concerning us. Certainly some scenes for our ministry are hard and trying; but they are the Lord's places, and somebody must fill them. And if we are called and appointed to them, they are as appropriate to us as to others.

---

[69] Jeremiah 1:7,8.

For myself, I have been singularly overruled and disappointed in the arrangement of my places of ministry all my way through. The places which I desired and sought have never been opened to me. I have been successively sent to places to which my tastes were repugnant and unexpectedly removed from places in which I had become contented and attached. Thus the Lord is pleased often to remove us from place to place, "from vessel to vessel, lest our taste remain in us."[70] And yet I have never failed to find, in subsequent experience, that the Lord's choice was the best choice; and the move which I had dreaded has been made graciously to open for me a happy, I might say, a still happier home.

I gave up the wealth of earth to preach the Savior's Gospel; and when I began that sacred work, in this world's goods I was poor enough. When I was settled in my first charge I had ten dollars in my possession, and that was borrowed. Through my whole early ministry, I knew much of the restraints of narrow means of living. I have had my full share of persecutions and hostilities. I know enough, in my personal experience, of the peculiar trials of the ministry. But I also know much of the unspeakable happiness of serving Jesus in his own appointed places, in this sacred work, with contentment and thanksgiving. And I must press this thought upon you, that, as an instrument of influence and usefulness with others, we need always a contented and cheerful temper. With this, though we are poor, we may make many rich.[71] A cheerful heart doeth good like a medicine.[72]

What a blessing such a pastor brings to the house of sorrow, to the chamber of sickness, to the abode of burdens and distress! His "countenance sharpeneth"[73] the hope, the patience, the endurance of all.

He comes every where as a fulfillment of joy. His visits are anticipated with delight. All rise up to call him blessed. The children and the "little ones" cling around him as a friend whom

---

[70] cf. Jeremiah 48:11.
[71] 2 Corinthians 6:10.
[72] Proverbs 17:22.
[73] Proverbs 27:17.

they love. All loving kindness, goodness, and truth are the spontaneous radiance from the character and life of such a man. In his path every valley is exalted, and every hill is made low; the crooked things become straight, and the rough places smooth.[74] It is a pleasure to contemplate the influence and the results of such a course.

But follow the history of a discontented, complaining man. What an unwholesome, repulsive miasma spreads around him! He can not be desired nor longed for nor tolerated but by those who are more truly the imitators of a mild and gentle Savior than he. He may know all books and all languages; he may be, in his own estimation, "wiser than Daniel," and really "prouder than Lucifer;" he may be an adept in all conversation and all culture; but none desire him, and every place in which his ministry is appointed and exercised becomes more really discontented than he.

Such a man occurs to my mind. He was talented, educated, and outwardly well prepared. But he had no aptitude of personal conformity to appointed conditions, and he has rolled and tumbled through the Church, from one inferior place to another still more so, until in age he seems likely to have no home open to him in any part of the Lord's work on earth. He asked me one day the reason for this. He said, " I preach the same truth as you. Why is my preaching useless?" We were near a butcher's stall filled with a stock of most attractive meat. "Why can not you eat that meat, so nicely cut up, and looking so clean?" I replied. "Why, it is not cooked," he said. "That is exactly the point," I answered. "That which is wanting in all your work is cooking—adaptation to the wants and condition of the people to whom you are sent. Your meat is nicely cut up and divided, but it is not cooked." It is a faithful, sympathizing, pastoral ministry which alone can make our public discourses really available, and prepare the food for the adequate nourishment of the people whom we are sent to feed.

---

[74] Isaiah 40:4.

John Newton once went to hear a very critical and accurate preacher; and when asked by him how he liked his discriminating analysis, answered, "One great distinction you seemed to have forgotten—the difference between bones and meat."

Now take these important INSTRUMENTS for your pastoral ministry, and go out with them to your work: Scriptural, evangelical, prayerful, exemplary, cheerful, contented, and conforming to the tastes and habits of others, with a loving, dignified accommodation. Eating that which is set before you—grateful for the hospitality of all; as open to the poor as to the rich; despising not the low degree; doing all in the name of the Lord Jesus, that he may be glorified in you. Thus he will make for you every lodging-place a Bethel, every host a Gaius, every wilderness a garden, in every place Onesiphorus and his house refreshing you, not ashamed of your chain. Be holy, faithful, happy, in your appointed work, and you will find households of faithful, happy ones around you, ministering to all your wants, grateful for all your teaching, blessing you in your arrival, thanking you in your departure, recalling you with pleasure, every where enlarging the circle of your prayer, and their supplication to include your names among those whom they remember before the throne of grace. "Such honor have all his saints."[75]

---

[75] Psalm 149:9.

# LECTURE FOUR

## THE AGENCIES AND OPPORTUNITIES

### OF THE PASTOR

### October 2, 1873

My young friends, a consideration of the OBJECT, the QUALIFI-
CATIONS, and the INSTRUMENTS of the Christian pastor
demanded in the nature and the prosecution of his work, leads
me now to ask your consideration of the AGENCIES and
OPPORTUNITIES which are prepared for him.

The distinction which I have made between instruments
and agencies will, I think, be immediately apparent to you.
Instruments or tools for a workman are personal possessions:
things which he brings to his appointed work. Agencies and
opportunities are characteristics of his appointed field of labor,
whatever it may be: the objects and the scenes upon which and
in connection with which he is to employ his instruments and
tools. He brings his own instruments to his work. He finds his
agencies and opportunities provided for him. His actual
usefulness and success depend upon a proper improvement of
his agencies with his instruments. An unskillful or unfurnished
workman will often destroy the best preparation for his success,
and a well-furnished and well-instructed workman will often
achieve a brilliant success with very limited and unpromising
provisions in his field of labor.

I. The first agency to which I will refer is PERSONAL VISITATION. By this, I mean not the occasional social visits of a Christian gentleman for his own comfort and pleasure, promotive as they may be of good fellowship and a friendly understanding in a community. I refer to direct, designed, and earnest personal effort to carry the ministry of the Gospel to every household, and to every soul committed to the care of a minister of Christ.

I well know the difficulty and the cost of maintaining the habit and the power of such a ministry. It demands all the living influence of true and active piety in a pastor's soul; all the love for Jesus and his cause which the Spirit of God has been pleased to bestow upon the pastor's heart: all the real interest in others, and love for the souls for whom the Savior died, which can be cultivated in the heart of man. But of the general demands and objects which are arrayed before the pastor's view and conscience, I have already sufficiently spoken. But the value of such an agency as that of which I now speak it is impossible to magnify.

The power of the Gospel, in its effective, spiritual ministry, is a personal power in the individual soul. The public preaching of the Gospel becomes really effectual only in the extent to which the Holy Spirit is pleased to carry its divine teaching, to govern and sanctify the inward nature of those who hear, with his own renewing power. But no really faithful preacher can stop his labors at this point of application. He must know his sheep, and call them by name; he must search out his flock, and carry the precious words of divine compassion and invitation to every house. His voice must thus be heard by all.

I concede to you, the labor of this is extreme. The wear and tear of nerves and affections is great. The obstacles and impediments to success are many. But notwithstanding all this, it remains a part of our appointed work, and an element of an imparted power. It is, indeed, the truly apostolic pattern of preaching, "Daily, and in every house, they ceased not to teach, and to preach Jesus Christ."[76] And it is an invaluable privilege to be permitted, and to be able, to carry it out systematically and constantly.

---

[76] Acts 5:42; cf. 20:19,20.

This bringing the Word of salvation and the voice of prayer to every house is most important in its direct effect upon the family we visit. It opens a welcome to our whole ministry; it entwines the affectionate sympathy of every heart around the person and character of the minister of Christ; it brings to each home, as their nearest and most cherished friend, the messenger of divine salvation; it presents him as one who understands and has experienced the power and the reality of this gift of God. And when such a ministry has been faithfully fulfilled, it must leave behind it a blessing from God upon the souls to whom this precious message has been so simply and affectionately presented.

Such a personal visitation gathers the attendance and the attention of all to the public stated congregation. I have known irreligious families, living wholly without a Sabbath and without God, thus won by the personal kindness of the minister to a constant attendance upon the public worship of the church, and to an abiding acceptance of the Gospel. The public instruction of the man whom they have learned to love becomes invested for them with an attraction and a power which they have never found before.

The effect of this personal work upon your own public ministry becomes most important. It furnishes you with practical material for preaching; it opens individual and social necessities for a special application of the Word of God; it transforms your general address to a distinct personal message; it converts the painted flame and glow of a mere lecture or harangue to the living fire of converting truth, around which the shivering and perishing will learn and love to gather, that they may be warmed and filled. "Come see a man who hath told me all things that ever I did"[77] becomes the repeated form upon many a tongue of a similar conviction.

You will rarely find such a visit from a truly sincere and friendly pastor to be rejected or under-valued. Take the instruments for your work which I have proposed,

---

[77] John 4:29.

understood by you in their use, tried by you in their experience, employed by you in the strength and love of your present Savior, persevering and repeated in your effort, and the Lord whom you serve will always open to you an effectual door, and many adversaries to the Gospel will be won over to be your chief friends.

II. In connection with this agency of personal visitation, you will generally find *a special opportunity* for your reception providentially prepared IN SEASONS OF PERSONAL SICKNESS AND DOMESTIC AFFLICTION. This is another agency divinely prepared. So antecedent to our personal work for Jesus are his provisions for us that our habitual experience discovers a way already prepared before us. Often when a hesitating, timorous man delays what seems to him a real call of personal duty, some unexpected opening, exhibiting a family waiting anxiously for an expected visit, will fill him with shame in a consciousness of his neglect. There are always open doors around us, and our duty is to seek them, and take advantage of them all.

When personal sickness lays by the active and the careless, or calls the child of God to bear the rod, and hear him who hath appointed it, there is a very manifest opening for our effort and our success. Our most precious seasons of approach to others will be when the world has been thus shut out, and there is time and opportunity to deliver our message in the Savior's name. All our appointed instruments of impression then come into use. We must be direct in our appeal, free and full in our utterance of the message of abounding grace and divine forgiveness. We go to offer the fullness of a Savior's merit and love to the acceptance of a waiting soul prepared to hear it. And we can not err on the side of sincere earnestness and affectionate encouragement to the weary, the wretched, and the lost. We can never magnify the blessings we may be permitted to receive in an assiduous and faithful ministry for Christ.

In one of my regular circuits of pastoral work, I passed the door of a household with whom I was quite familiar, but of whom I had heard nothing of particular distress. Four physicians' carriages were standing at the door. I stopped to ask the cause. The father of the family had been suddenly found the subject of a virulent cancer in the face, the reality of which he had never suspected. The consultation determined that no medical power could rescue or restore him. And he was left to meet an inevitable death.

Here was my provided opportunity. I called immediately after the departure of the physicians, as the messenger of divine teaching and encouragement. Four months of wasting and exhaustion I witnessed in an unceasing progress. But a most precious preparation of grace and divine goodness I was permitted also to see. The disease was fearful—but the grace was most abundant. He lived from week to week in agony. But he was led on from joy to joy by the Spirit of God. When I supposed him near the close of his career, though still maintaining conversation with entire intelligence, he said to me, "Oh, do you not see him?"—pointing his finger over the foot of his bed—"do you not see him?" "See whom?" I said. "Oh, Jesus. There he is; there he stands. How glorious! He has come for me—I shall go with him." I could see nothing peculiar in the direction to which he pointed. But his whole pain-worn, half-eaten countenance was filled with joy. That night in his sleep he departed without a pang, and without the consciousness of the friends who were watching around him. Other similar scenes I have also seen in different portions of my ministry, giving incidental illustrations at least of the precious words of our Lord, "I will come again and receive you unto myself."[78]

Two years' constant pastoral visiting to a faithful "daughter of the Lord Almighty," departing in a lingering consumption, were closed, when vocal speech had gone, by

---

[78] John 14:3.

a most affectionate testimony of gratitude in the very night of her departure. Drawing my ear closely to her lips, with her wasted arm around my neck, she whispered, "Jesus will bless you for all that you have done for me, and all that you have told me of him. You can never know in this world how much I have loved you."

Such providences as these I call peculiar preparations for our work. I consider them a special *agency*, of which we are to take advantage. I could employ many hours in relating to you similar illustrations which have been graciously given to me. I present them to you for your guidance. Be ready for them. Expect them. Take advantage of them. Go out for Jesus, sympathizing, intelligent, experienced messengers of his Word, with the glad tidings of a Savior's work complete and power divine; of a divine forgiveness, absolute and free. Be patient. Be cheerful. Be encouraging. Be sympathizing. Let the very tones of your voice be a comfort and a blessing. Let your whole manner be simple, real, earnest, hopeful. Strive to establish an entire confidence, communion, between yourselves and those whom you visit. An untender, unsympathizing manner can have no good effect. A subservient, cringing manner can have no more. We shrivel up, corrugated, before a hard and cold address. We doubt the reality of a whining, sing-song one. Go, in the spirit of your divine Master, dignified but gentle; knowing what you say, and what to say; and he will bless you. If you assume a lofty, pretentious style—scolding, rebuking, censuring—you will do no good; you will shut against yourselves every door which he may open.

This is a very important subject for you to consider. It is a great thing to learn how to deliver your Lord's message simply, freely, positively, to suffering souls. We do not go in this divinely prepared agency to offer a conditional hope, or to describe a way in which the human soul may reconstruct itself. We go to tell to others that which our Lord has told to us; and the truth and power of which he has made us to understand and feel. Divine inspiration has taught us, and made us partakers of the heavenly benefit. The message to a lost sinner is not, God will save you, if you obey and love him. It is, God has accomplished a perfect salvation; believe, trust, and love him. It is this salvation, accomplished and perfect, by the power and in the fullness of an Almighty Savior, which you are sent to proclaim. The real power of the ministry is in the simple, believing delivery of this message, and our free offer of this salvation.

We go to tell others that which God has taught us—intelligence of inestimable worth to all who are ready to hear and to receive it. It is the declaration of God's own reconciliation, and of man's complete salvation, in the obedience and death of the Lord Jesus Christ. We present gracious invitations, which are and must be either gratefully accepted or rebelliously rejected by all who hear, and that at once. The alternative is Christ or no Christ—life or death. We can not say that the message may not be again repeated. But so far as each present message goes, there is the result and the end.

I was once called late in the evening to visit a young man at a boarding-house in Philadelphia. He was an officer in the United States Army, returning from the Florida War, on his way to his Northern home. He was extremely ill. I took him by the hand, and told him of this work and love of Jesus, this great salvation and victory for him, in the precious blood of the Son of God. He started from me with a scream. "Oh, do not talk to me about that. That was just what my mother used to tell me; but I would not hear her. It is too late—too late now." I tried in vain to persuade him to hear me. I knelt by his side, and prayed to that gracious Savior who alone could hear and bless. The young man turned his face away from me, and covered his head, and cried aloud, "Oh, go away—leave me. There is no hope now." It was midnight, and I retired. At daylight I was there again. The crape upon the bell-pull told me that all was over. The nurse said he was quiet till his departure, and said no more. God only could tell if the message had been effective through his abounding grace.

But thus we go forth, like the visitor in the Catacombs, with this single thread in our hands. If we lose this, all is lost. We have no other message. We can not go beyond the Word of the Lord to say less or more. Each visit may be our last opportunity. We are always standing on the line between two worlds. Eternity may hang upon the single message which we now deliver. What an agency is this! What an opportunity! What a responsibility is involved in it! Every moment and every word becomes increasingly precious; and a loving, experienced pastor will deeply feel the solemnity of the crisis and of his fidelity therein.

But this providential agency extends far beyond occasional seasons of personal sickness and domestic affliction. Our whole field of appointed labor is a special providence for us. We are selected messengers from God wherever we are sent. There is some particular reason why we have been individually directed to the particular community in which, by a power beyond our own choice, our lot has been cast. It is a very low and inadequate view of our ministry for Christ to consider it in any sense a mere chosen profession, the duties and advantages of which are a subject of our own will, and of our personal selection. I have not been willing to esteem myself less personally or distinctly sent to a particular community, or removed from one place to another for my appointed work, than the first generation of the apostles, or the present missionaries of the Gospel to a foreign land. The reality of our power and usefulness in this great work is very essentially bound up with our consciousness of this divine appointment and divine message. The whole aspect and peculiar distinctions of the persons to whom our ministry has been directed are really for us a providential arrangement, especially prepared for our work; and we must endeavor to conform our efforts for others, and our own tastes, habits, and contentment, amid the duties of our calling, to the facts which seem so clearly to indicate the will of God concerning us.

The man in the quietness and self-control of a retired, rural, country place, where he may command his own time, and occupy himself in his work according to his own choice and habits, in the calm routine of an unnoticed life; and the same man in a crowded, bustling city, where he is the subject of laws, habits, conveniences, beyond his own will or possible power to influence, becomes, if he succeed in his work, really two different men. Many a one, whose youthful bark was first launched upon the tranquil surface of an inland lake, where all motion was moderate and peaceful, and the whole circumference encircling him was within his own sight, when he becomes tossed upon the unresting surges of a sea which he has no power to control—when his own safety or ability to get through is often the one question which absorbs his mind—looks back with an intense desire to be once more as he was in former days, and to feel once more as he felt when he was not the slave of an ungovernable pressure, but the ruler of an unbroken repose.

We can never get through this variety of experience creditably or happily, usefully or honorably, unless we can realize the fact that we are not our own; our place and circumstances of ministry are not under our own direction; but as it is our commanding, unchanging decision in every thing thoroughly to obey the will of our divine Lord. That gracious Will holds us in the hollow of his hand; fixes the bounds of our habitation; gives us the borders of our dwelling; and teaches us in his own way the special message which we are to deliver, amid these agencies of his own devising.

We are thus, from the beginning to the end of life, the messengers of the Lord of Hosts to our fellow-men; whether to the quiet and comparatively orderly population of a rural district, or to the driving, swelling crowd of a populous city; to the comparatively limited knowledge of the families of the poor, or to the assuming or real distinctions and elevations of the educated and the rich. We are every where the selected and appointed ministers of the Lord Jesus Christ, and are to be contented to be in the world, as he was in the world.

The one primary, fundamental object of our ministry, never to be forgotten, is the promotion of the personal glory of our divine Lord. The final, satisfying accomplishment of our controlling desire will be the establishment of his authority and the glory of his kingdom. In order to this, and for the attainment of this, our duty, our absorbing purpose, is to be the individual conversion of the souls of men to him, in whom alone there is life for the perishing and the lost. We shall unceasingly seek their edification in the knowledge and love of him; and their walk in newness and holiness of life, under the guidance of his Spirit, and in the pattern and beauty of his example. For this great work we are on earth among the living. For this we have solemnly given ourselves to Jesus as our Lord. Renouncing all other authority and will, we look to him to send whom he will send; to send where he will send; and to accomplish his gracious work in his own way. And whether our individual field be laid out among the rich or the poor, the elevated or the low, the educated or the ignorant, the single purpose of our mind and choice will be to glorify Jesus, and to work for him alone.

The appointment of our scene of labor is the providence of that Great Ruler who holdeth the stars in his right hand.[79] You will allow me to illustrate the apparent directions of this providence by some occurrences in my own experience. At twenty-one years of age and a few weeks over, I left my New England home in the character of a preacher—the world before me and Providence my guide. Four weeks afterward I found myself settled as a pastor in a church in Georgetown, in the District of Columbia, then the business suburb of the city of

---

[79] Revelation 1:16,20; 2:1.

Washington. It was a church of which I had never heard, and in which not a single individual was known to me. They accidentally heard me, without my knowledge. Their aged pastor left them but the Sunday previous, and pleasantly said to them, "If that young man had an H in his name, he would be the very *thing* for you." They took me at his word, and thus made me the thing. It was a largely intelligent and cultivated audience. I had written very little. My habit of preaching, which I had acquired in a revival at Bristol, Rhode Island, from whence I had gone within the previous month, was entirely extemporaneous, and was sometimes very trying. But I could not avoid the conclusion that I had been sent to this place, and I could not cherish the thought of flinching or running. It proved the opening to my whole life's work, and gave me in the very morning of my youth the opportunity of an extended acquaintance which I could hardly have expected to attain. A large portion of the members of Congress at that time boarded in Georgetown.

It was here that an incident occurred which I have seen in print, and to which I will therefore refer. On one Sunday I went as usual to my church, with my feeble preparation for the pulpit. It was during the session of Congress, and, to my amazement, a large number of public men were there, many of whom were personal friends of my father. I was terrified beyond control at the sight, and my gracious Lord left me to my own pride for my chastening. I forgot my text and my whole subject. And after blundering on for perhaps ten minutes in a most profuse perspiration, overwhelmed with confusion, I suddenly closed the service and dismissed the congregation. Walking home, bowed down with my mortification, my wife, a daughter of Bishop Griswold, said to me: "Now do give up this attempt at extemporaneous preaching. You know my father said it would always be desultory and unconnected. You will never succeed in it, I fear." I replied, "I will never give it up. This very occasion has made me determined. It can be acquired, and, by the Lord's help, I

will acquire it." Thirty years after that, I saw Mr. Van
Buren, who was one of my distinguished hearers on that
day, in St. George's Church in the City of New York. He
came up to the chancel to speak to me, with his friend
Judge Vanderpoel, whom he was visiting. Referring to some
things past, I said, "Do you remember that day of my
dreadful failure in preaching, in Georgetown, in the
beginning of my ministry?" "Oh yes," said he; "but you
have never failed since."

My two years' ministry in Georgetown opened to me a
country field of labor in a very rich section of Southern
Maryland. I was called to a parish which I had never heard
of, through some persons who had heard me in
Georgetown, resident in that country. The people had the
reputation of great wealth and of fearful dissipation. They
were the owners of near three thousand slaves. The
opening was so unsought and providential that I
determined to accede to their request. An older minister,
who knew the place, said to me: "Well, Tyng, I will give you
six months there. They will never stand *you*." I passed with
them six happy years; and when, most unwillingly, I left
them to remove to Philadelphia, they gathered around me
with the appeal, "Why *do* you leave us? You might spend
your life with us. We will do any thing for you; we shall
never get another minister that we shall like so much." And
yet, by the help of my gracious Lord, I did not truckle to
their habits of life. I preached in their taverns and from
house to house, wherever I could find a room or a
gathering for the purpose.

Of some of my early sermons to this people in one of
the taverns, I will repeat to you my texts. Isaiah 3:9, "The
show of their countenance doth witness against them; and
they declare their sin as Sodom, they hide it not. Woe unto
their soul, for they have rewarded evil unto themselves."
Isaiah 5:11-14, "Woe unto them that rise up early in the
morning, that they may follow strong drink; that continue
until night, till wine inflame them. But they regard not the

work of the Lord, neither consider the operation of his hands. Therefore hell hath enlarged herself, and opened her mouth without measure: and their glory, and their multitude, and their pomp, and he that rejoiceth, shall descend into it." Ezekiel 16:49, "Behold, this was the iniquity of Sodom: pride, fullness of bread, and abundance of idleness was in her and in her daughters; therefore I took them away as I saw good."

There was at first a good deal of bustling and some threats, under these direct rebukes of their prevailing sins. But I yielded nothing. And the complaints ended, under the counsel of an old resident, who said: "You had better let that young man alone. You will not do much with him, and you know he is right."

God gave me many precious souls among that people even some who were the most repulsive at the beginning. And their kind remembrance of me has been perpetuated among their children and their grandchildren, of which, after the passage of fifty years, I have lately received a very gratifying expression and evidence.

I could illustrate this providential agency by many successive facts in the cities of Philadelphia and New York; but I have not time nor space for them here. I trust you will not deem it mere personal vanity which leads me to refer to these individual facts. Our providences are all our own— and they are often very precious gifts of God. The gracious Lord, who so wonderfully prepares our way in his work, must have the honor of all that minute and gracious care with which he directs our steps. But we must not be unmindful in its observation, nor silent in its acknowledgment.

III. Beyond these two aspects of agencies, prepared for our work, there is THE AGENCY OF SOCIAL RELIGIOUS MEETINGS OF VARIOUS DESCRIPTIONS. These must habitually make up an important portion of our pastoral work in every week. In connection with our regular Sabbath work faithfully maintained, they constitute an indispensable element of success in the fulfillment of our responsibility as pastors in the Church of our gracious Lord.

These varied religious meetings are so familiar to our knowledge in the various churches of the Lord, whether as conference or class or prayer meetings, that I feel no necessity laid upon me for an attempted exposition of their character. I have been familiar with their usefulness, and in my various fields of labor have always desired to maintain them, as far as the providential circumstances around me would permit. In our different fields of labor, there is a great difference in the facility of establishing these social meetings, and the ease with which they may be sustained.

But it is habitually through them that much of a pastor's personal relations to the individual members of his flock, and his acquaintance with their religious condition and necessities, are inaugurated and made available. A wise and skillful pastor will always throw his whole influence and mental attainments into these openings for the revival and prosperity of the power of the Gospel among the people. They furnish him an opportunity for special personal instruction, for the discrimination and correction of local and occasional errors and evils, for the cultivation of the special, personal fruits of practical religion, and for familiar expositions of the Word of God, for which he can find no time or opportunity in the public services of the Sabbath.

These familiar meetings are the occasion for calling forth, for the service of the Gospel, hidden talent and experience in the minds of laymen, which may be made of great value in the more public work of the Lord. When they are thus faithfully and affectionately sustained by the whole power of the pastor's influence and personal aid, they are a preparation for the gracious revivals in the Church, and the special gifts of the Spirit of the Lord with which it pleases God, according to his own will, to bless and edify his people. There is much pure gold concealed by the routine of earthly occupation among the members of the Church, which the skillful pastor may thus bring forth for the

Savior's honor. It should be the desire of his heart that all the Lord's people might be prophets.[80] A true and faithful minister of Christ will never cultivate or allow an unreasonable jealousy of lay influence, nor fear the undue exaltation of those whom God hath called and blessed.

Not long since I was present at the public worship of two churches of different names on the Sabbath, in neither of which did I hear a distinct or edifying Gospel message. In the evening I went to the Methodist congregation, where, in the absence of the appointed pastor, a young local preacher was officiating. From him I heard a simple, faithful, precious sermon on the priesthood of Jesus, which filled me with thankfulness and joy. At the close of the worship, I went up to the young man, and thanked him for his very acceptable service. He replied, "You do not know me, but I know you well. You have been awfully in my way tonight." I said, "I thought so, my dear young friend, by the way in which you have been firing through me in your sermon. Bless the Lord, that he gives you grace to speak so truly and so usefully to his people." In this lay effort, you should be always glad. You have nothing to fear from the assumption or exaltation of these services. If they are likely to tread upon your heels, let it excite you to new efforts to keep your undisputed place as leaders in the real work of the Lord.

IV. I pass to a fourth agency, which the Lord has prepared for every faithful pastor in his Church. I mean THE CARE AND THE CULTIVATION OF THE YOUTH OF HIS FLOCK.[81] The possibility of bringing religious truth

---

[80] Numbers 11:29.

[81] We would strongly recommend several of our own titles on the subject of pastoral ministry to the children and young people of the congregation. First, we urge reading *For the Work of the Ministry* by William G. Blaikie (pp. 194-205), *Homiletics and Pastoral Theology* by William G.T. Shedd (pp. 356-375); and second, the works of John Todd, Richard Newton, T.H. Gallaudet and J.W. Alexander. Each of these men wrote books for the instruction of the young which can serve as a model for the modern day Gospel Minister. These books are a gold-mine of resources to assist you in seeking to communicate the Word of God to the children of your flock.

effectually to the mind and acceptance of children, and the bringing of children, in a real experience of its power, to the knowledge of a Savior, and to an intelligent enjoyment of all the privileges of the Christian household, has been an attainment of the present generation of the Church. I ought, indeed, more properly and truly to say, has been a gracious gift and revelation to the Church in our time and our observation.

We are in a period of divine teaching and government, in which a very large proportion, perhaps even a majority, of the accessions to the Church of Christ are among the children of the household: "The feeble one is as David; and the lame taketh the prey."[82] This has been to me a fact, in my observation and experience, of the deepest interest. I commenced my ministry with little opportunity for this observation. Our old New England education was one of law and duty, not of privilege and encouragement. The right thing was presented as obligatory, not attractive. The fear of fanaticism, and of the hazardous exaltation of youth and ignorance, was a prevailing feeling. We were taught in our childhood a dry and technical catechism, the very terms of which it was impossible to understand. But the conversion of children, their real turning, in heart and life, to the love and service of Jesus, would have been almost esteemed an impertinence, or a whim not to be allowed or regarded.

This was not from an unwillingness that children should be really right and good, but from a fear of violating old and inherited custom and order: attended with much possible evil, and with no probable advantage. Religious attention was not directed to Biblical teaching for childhood. Indeed, Bibles were so scarce and inaccessible upon any large basis, and Sunday-schools were so perfectly unknown, that there were comparatively no Bibles within the reach of children for their use. The first Bible which I ever personally owned I bought with my pocket-money, at

---

[82] Zechariah 12:8.

eleven years of age, at Andover Academy. I then gave one dollar and a quarter for a small, plain English Bible, and for which we now pay less than a fifth of that sum.

But a remarkable change has taken place in public sentiment and public experience. We are now living to see Christian childhood made the conceded right, the cherished anticipation, perhaps I might say, the habitual expectation of the Church of God. Our Sunday-schools, in their extension of familiar Biblical instruction; in their connecting mature love for Jesus, in kind and experienced teachers, with the multitudes of opening youthful minds; in their uniting earnest prayer and direct effort, by conversation and instruction, for the immediate, manifest conversion of children; in their vast extension of Biblical and evangelical knowledge among the children of the Church, have been made the instruments of introducing an entirely new era in the relation of children to the Church of God.

The effect has been widely manifested. The Gospel, both in its teaching and in its requisitions, has been made attractive to youthful minds. Pastors and mature Christians have become convinced that scarce any intelligent childhood is too young to understand the love of Jesus; the happiness of serving him; the evidence and experience of real conversion to him; or to give the clearest testimony and account of their personal experience of the transforming power of the Holy Spirit in its distinguishing evidences and results.

I have received to the Lord's Table whole classes of youth, the precious seals to faithful teachers' usefulness and acceptance in this blessed work. I should make no period of youth an objection, where I could receive the testimony of personal conversion and Christian experience so clear and convincing as I have found it in many hundreds of these fruits of faithful teaching in the Word of God. Perhaps the youngest actual communicant I have received may have been ten years of age. I should not be willing to establish any arbitrary standard of age in this relation. Some of the most clear and remarkable fruits of living, intelligent faith in Jesus I have found in a literal infantile piety.[83]

More than fifty ministers of the Gospel of the Lord Jesus I have seen come forth from this early teaching in the precious truth and love of a divine Savior. I might say that to me the habitual, normal shape of a true profession of Christ has almost established itself in this influence upon youth. While I dare not exclude any from personal hope whom the Lord is pleased to teach and to accept, even in the last days of age, my hope in the ministry, and my experience of its actual gathering, have, in a great degree, settled down to the youth of my flock, with but here and there a person of adult or advanced age, as monuments that God has not altogether forsaken those who have repelled his gracious offers in their earlier age.

To carry out this experience of the past in my anticipations of the future, I cherish my opportunities to foster in every way the Sunday-schools of my church. I have always given one half of the Sabbath's public teaching expressly to the young, upon subjects in the Scriptures which are adapted to interest them, and in language which they can readily understand. The abounding grace of the Lord Jesus has remarkably blessed my efforts in this important work, and given me much to comfort me in all these years of completed labor which he has permitted me to lay at his feet.

The whole effect of this gracious, providential agency in our day has been an extension and enlargement of Christian knowledge, and adaptation to Christian labor, which have elevated the whole standard of demand upon the preparation, the intelligence, the earnestness, and the real devotion of the Gospel ministry. You will start, in the

---

[83] Please note our title, *Early Piety Illustrated: The Memoir of Nathan Dickerman* by Gorham Abbott. This is the true account of the conversion and death-bed faith of a little sufferer who died before his eighth birthday. It is a most moving testimony of the power of the Gospel in a young life. It is a tragedy that many Gospel Ministers seem to think it impossible for young children to grasp the truth in their early years. This book will challenge the low view of "infantile piety" in our dark day.

very opening of your course, upon a far higher plane of demand and of attainment than we, who have gone so long before you, imagined possible in the beginning of our day. You must cultivate and maintain a spirit and purpose to work up to this rising standard of intelligence and requisition.

There is in our time another apparent enlargement of intellectual claim, at least, which is like moonlight, indefinitely revealing, but giving no heat and no life; which becomes the area for human pride, for skepticism, and indifference to all truth, its inseparable companion. This is a flippant, boastful, Jehu temper, which overturns more carriages than it safely drives, and injures far more than it has power to guide to any security or peace.

I advise you to waste no time in an attempted arguing with this opposing spirit. Preach your gracious Master's positive and unchangeable message, whether men will hear, or whether they will forbear. Be ready to give a clear reason for your own hope to those who ask you with meekness and fear.[84] As John Newton proposed, fill your basket so completely with wheat that Satan may find no opportunity to occupy it with his chaff. Anticipate in your ministry all the arts and efforts of the Evil One, by a clear, constant, earnest effort: to gather childhood in a living consecration to the Savior, and to win the youth to whom the Lord shall send you to the knowledge and love of his Word.

Remember that adversaries are nothing when the Lord is on your side. Paul gloried in the opposition of a surrounding world. He called it "an open door,"[85] where there were "many adversaries." A head-wind to the steamer enhances the power of the furnace, and increases the rapidity and momentum of the ship. With all controversy, as well as without it, "godliness is a great gain."[86] David was never more happy than when he could say to Saul: "Thy servant kept his

---

[84] 1 Peter 3:15.
[85] 1 Corinthians 16:9; cf. 2 Corinthians 2:12; Colossians 4:3.
[86] 1 Timothy 4:8.

father's sheep, and there came a lion and a bear, and took a lamb out of the flock. And I went after him, and delivered it out of his mouth. And when he rose against me, I caught him by his beard, and smote him and slew him."[87] These lambs of Jesus are entrusted to your care. "Feed them,"[88] he says. "Take care of them; and whatsoever thou spendest, when I return I will repay thee."[89] Learn to feed them *simply*, appropriately. An old farmer said of an unintelligible preacher whom he heard, "When will these men give up trying to feed sheep out of horse-racks." There is nothing in the Bible which the plainest of your hearers can not understand, if you speak to them in language which they can comprehend. Often the apparently least intellectual among the souls committed to you, you will find "mighty in the Scriptures,"[90] from an habitual feeding on the Word of God.

Deal with them *kindly*. Be never hasty or cross in manner or expression. Remember it was the sunshine, and not the north wind, which stripped the traveler's cloak from him. Kind words, a soft answer, do good like a medicine.[91]

Never be *impatient*. You will have narrow necks to fill. And the gentle dropping of the tea-kettle will be far better and more successful than the swashing of the pump.

Be really *loving*. Children are quick detectors of reality in feeling. A Christ-loving pastor will be always a child-loving pastor. The real victory over a young heart is a castle for your life.

Pray for the young. Pray with them in language perfectly simple, in terms expressive. Lay aside your grandeur, and be yourselves little children with them. They will cling to the knees which have bent with them before the throne. You can never have a happier ministry than this. And if you are truly faithful in it, you will get in the affection and faithfulness of the young of your flock a most abundant reward.

---

[87] 1 Samuel 17:34,35.
[88] John 21:15-17.
[89] Luke 10:35.
[90] Acts 18:24.
[91] Proverbs 17:22.

The AGENCIES which I have thus specified, as prepared for the pastor's work, are but a selection from the number which might be referred to. Such preparations present most important openings for usefulness and success in this work. In personal visitation, in providential openings, in social meetings, in care and love for the young, you will have presented to you a large and most available field for a pastor's thought and care and effort. And when you bring into connection with these prepared AGENCIES your own appointed and sanctioned INSTRUMENTS, your real and manifest QUALIFICATIONS, the one great OBJECT of your pastoral work in the conversion of souls to CHRIST will prosper in your hands, and Jesus your Lord will be glorified in your ministry for him.

In closing this special portion of our proposed course, let me again press upon you, as the one great, controlling fact in your history—you can do nothing for the Savior but in the degree and in the reality in which he dwells by his own Spirit in you. "Abide in me," is his one discriminating precept for you. "He that abideth in me, and I in him, the same bringeth forth much fruit. Separate from me, ye can do nothing."[92]

This great principle of life and conduct we need to have impressed upon us every day anew. We are alive when we live in Christ. We are mighty through him. We can do all things through him that strengtheneth us.[93] In his fellowship, in his light, with his voice encouraging, his arm upholding, his love soothing, his smile repaying, we can go through every trial with perfect peace. We can endure all losses with abiding, abounding joy. We can pass through the valley of the shadow of death, and fear no evil.

In all your pastoral work carry this great remembrance with you: "He will guide you with his counsel, and afterward receive you to his glory."[94] The days which you have given to his service on the earth, never to be forgotten, shall bloom in an immortal memory—shall shine with an everlasting light in the presence of your Lord; and shall live in the grateful minds of hundreds,

[92] John 15:4,5.
[93] Philippians 4:13.
[94] Psalm 73:24.

perhaps of thousands, who have been guarded, guided, fed, and nurtured by you for the glory of him who will be their Lord and your Lord in an eternal life.

# LECTURE FIVE

## THE POWER AND ATTAINMENTS

### OF THE PASTOR

#### October 3, 1873

My young friends, I am grateful for the attention which you have given to the four lectures already heard. I come now to conclude my appointed course with a consideration of the elements of POWER, and the real ATTAINMENTS of the Christian pastor, whose faithful ministry in this important field we have thus far followed. These illustrations of actual power and attainment I shall endeavor to place upon that which I should esteem a moderate ground, and within the reach and the enjoyment of every truly faithful young man in the ministry of Christ. I shall confine myself to the platform of thought and suggestion which we have already laid out. We shall thus he able to bring the points of our previous consideration to their proper and adequate result.

I. The first element of power in the exercise of this pastoral ministry which I will mention is THE *SIMPLICITY* OF THE TRUTH OF GOD WHICH THE FAITHFUL PASTOR CARRIES WITH HIM. I have adduced as the first instrument to be employed in his work, "the Word of God *thoroughly believed;*" that is, really incorporated and employed as unquestionable truth in the mind and thought of the man who ministers it.

The Christian pastor's visit is a provided place and opportunity for instruction, guidance, and individual consolation and relief for those to whom he ministers. It is not a scene for discussion or controversy, or attempted argument, or any unsettling influence upon the minds which he thus addresses. That is a beautiful divine description of the pastor's work and office in which the prophet describes the appointed work for him who was to be the Chief Shepherd of this chosen flock: "The Spirit of the Lord God is upon me, because the Lord hath anointed me to preach good tidings unto the meek. He hath sent me to bind up the broken-hearted, to proclaim liberty to the captives, and the opening of the prison to them that are bound; to proclaim the acceptable year of the Lord, and the day of vengeance of our God; to comfort all that mourn; to appoint unto them that mourn in Zion, to give unto them beauty for ashes, the oil of joy for mourning, and the garment of praise for the spirit of heaviness."[95]

This is a very precise and affecting description of a faithful pastor's daily work in the measure and degree in which man can realize and fulfill it. In this work we are to employ the inspired Word of God as his infallible and undeniable truth. We must be familiar with its contents. We must have its instructions and testimonies laid up in our memory and mind. We must remember that it is in itself the Word of the Holy Ghost—the life-giving Word. The power is in the WORD.

As we sit by the sick, as we strive to elevate the sorrowing and the depressed, as we attempt to guide the inquiring or to direct the anxious, our power is not in our own skill or wisdom or experience, but in the truth and testimony of the Word itself. God's words are better than ours. His own language in our instruction, or our prayer, will be the instrument of his own divine blessing. A single passage or sentence of this precious Word will sometimes be impressed upon the conscience and the memory of those to whom we minister, as "with the point of the diamond, and like lead in the rock forever."[96]

The pastor who is the most completely furnished with this gracious Word, and who employs it the most simply and

---

[95] Isaiah 61:1-3.
[96] Jeremiah 17:1.

constantly in his ministry, will always be the most effective and useful messenger for the Lord of Hosts to the secret, personal wants of a suffering people. His mind thoroughly alive with the sacred language, will quickly pass, like a bird upon the tree, from promise to promise, from one precious utterance to another, in the repetition and application of God's precious truth—the living Word which abideth forever.[97] And his whole ministry will be made a life-giving ministry to those for whom he thus labors in the Lord's name. Our usefulness in this work is not in the wisdom of men, but in the power of God.

II. A second element of our power is in OUR OWN CLEAR PERCEPTION AND UTTERANCE OF THIS DISCRIMINATED, SACRED TRUTH. Effective skill in employing and applying the inspired Word of God is a very precious and important gift. This is not the fruit of peculiar intellectual grasp or acquisition, nor the result of varied learning in Biblical criticism or the languages and emendations of the Word. It is in the clear discernment and experience of its divine power and purpose; in a full understanding of the scheme of divine grace and the salvation of man, which these holy writings contain and proclaim.

Knowledge and experience of human suffering, and practical sympathy in applying the messages of the sacred Word to the personal wants and sufferings of those to whom we minister, is an eminent instrument of power. In the hands of two different men, discriminated by this one element of distinction, the Bible seems an entirely different book. The power which the pastor exercises who can sit by the bedside of the sick, or in the circle of the sorrowing, and without formality, or pretense, or assumed solemnity of manner, can clearly, distinctly, gently utter the language of the Spirit, in an exposition of the privileges of grace, and the way of divine salvation which the Word of God contains, can not be transcended by any other exercise of the Christian ministry. "Sanctify them by the truth," the Savior said; "Thy Word is truth."[98]

---

[97] 1 Peter 1:23.
[98] John 17:17.

Make it your constant purpose and effort to gain clear and comprehensive views of the divine instructions; distinct perceptions of the practical use and design of the words of eternal life. Seek an enlightened apprehension of the glory of the Savior's person; of the facts of his history; of the perfectness of his obedience for man; of the fullness of his reconciling sacrifice; of the glorious reality of his resurrection, and his eternal reign; of his personal relation to his people, as their one justification and their glorious recompense of reward; their inseparable companion on earth; their life and their portion forever. Learn to teach and to preach in your pastor work of Jesus only—of Jesus clearly and discriminately; as really understanding the whole scheme and fullness of his grace, and knowing whereof you affirm. Here is a power which will never fail you.

A younger successor of mine in the ministry, visiting an old and wasting widow in the congregation, asked her what he should do for her. "Only tell me a little more of Jesus, as my old pastor used to," was her significant reply.

How often have I heard the poor, the aged, the ignorant of this world, in the midst of sorrow, suffering, and death, glorifying their Savior, with such strong and perfect faith, with such clear intelligence and perception of his work and worth, that their utterance and knowledge seemed like a direct inspiration from God.

There is your element of power. You do not prevail with the hearts of your people by expostulations, or reproofs, or earnestness of appeal alone. Jesus is the Bread of Life; and you must feed your hungering ones with that Living Bread. If you go upon your pastor work, carrying this clear perception, this simple faith, this calm and steadfast confidence in the revelation of a Savior's person, work, and power, you will have utterance given to you. Jesus will make you mighty to prevail. And you will find this Scriptural simplicity of teaching an element of constant and very precious influence for the promotion of his glory and the success of your work.

III. A third element of power in your pastor work will be YOUR MANIFEST EXPERIENCE AND ENJOYMENT OF THE

TRUTH YOU TEACH. Let your fire be real—the flame of the Holy Spirit burning on the altar of your own converted, believing soul, never to go out day or night. No sight can be more sad than to see a spiritually blind, unconverted man attempting to minister to the sick and suffering, the awakened and inquiring. Such a one in my acquaintance was desired to visit a lady in his own congregation, under deep conviction of sin. His first opening address to her was, "Miss B., I understand you have been thinking of eternity." "I have thought much of it," she replied. "Would you like to have me ask the Rev. Mr. P. to visit you?" naming another minister of a more serious character. "No, sir," she answered. "If my own minister can not guide me in the way of salvation, my Bible will."

Another of the same character, known to me, was called to visit a sick lady. Standing at the door of her chamber, he said, "Will you have the Communion, or only the Visitation?" "Not the Communion this morning," she answered. He took his Prayer-book from his pocket, and read the Office for the Visitation of the Sick, and departed.

We may well ask, 'How can a ministry so formal and lifeless be an adequate ministry of the Gospel to the souls of men?' "Taste yourselves, that the Lord is gracious."[99] Be you alive unto God, in Jesus Christ our Lord, in your own personal experience of his life-giving power. Let the words you speak be written and engraved by the Holy Spirit in your own hearts, and know what you say and whereof you affirm. There is a power in such a ministry which every one feels, and which none are ready to deny. The pastor evidently "leads the way;" and he is relied upon with confidence, and received with welcome and reverence.

Such a pastor is at home in every household. He is cherished by every true child of God. The family of the Lord are really fed by him, and welcome his coming in the very spirit of the prophetic description: "How beautiful upon the mountains are the feet of him that bringeth good tidings, that publisheth

---

[99] Psalm 34:8.

peace; that publisheth salvation; that saith unto Zion, 'Thy God reigneth.'"[100] This is the power which will attend a manifest, real experience of the Gospel, which as pastors of the Savior's flock you are employed to teach.

IV. Another element of power will be found in YOUR HABIT OF PERSONAL, INWROUGHT PRAYER. This power of prayer may be considered in its twofold exercise: in your own personal communion with God your Savior, bringing your divine strength and guidance from him; and in your social prayer with others, making you the instrument of imparting strength from God to them.

The truly faithful pastor lives in prayer. It is the controlling purpose—the habitual exercise and employment of his life. He loves to go alone within the veil to have a blessed fellowship, a personal converse with the God of his salvation. He habitually returns to bless his people with the blessings with which he has been enriched by God his Savior.

He is accustomed to lay the cares, the wants, the condition of his people before the throne of an exalted Savior. The many questions which he has not skill to answer, the many difficulties which he has no power to relieve, the names and the necessities of those committed to him, he frequently recounts before the mercy-seat of God, as Aaron carried the names of the tribes of Israel engraven on his heart with the power of a living affection. And he receives a new power for his ministry which is the gift of God, and which enables him to deal successfully with cases of trial which were before beyond his reach, insoluble by any wisdom of his own. If you would be truly faithful and useful pastors to the flock of Jesus, you will find here one most important and indispensable element of a desired and needed power in your work.

But I also wish to speak of the exercise and habit of prayer *with others,* in your personal visits as pastors. You will find such exercises to be most welcome, valued, precious seasons, and instruments of divine blessing upon your people. I well know the

[100] Isaiah 52:7.

difficulties which are frequently apparently in the way of your proposal of such an exercise in your personal visits. But far more generally than you imagine, the expectation is cherished by others with pleasure; and the disappointment is real, when the desire has not been met by you. As a rule in this peculiar crisis, the obstacle is far more generally in the fear and the sensitive shrinking of the minister than in the hostility of the people. A truly prayerful, faithful minister will always find an open door.

Dr. Edward Payson[101] was invited to an evening entertainment in a family and circle of friends, where the master of the house was very averse to the minister's habit of social prayer, and had his table so arranged as to prevent the expected proposal. Dr. Payson said to him, in his gentle way, "Who was it, sir, that said these standing feasts were contrived by Satan, to shut out the asking for a divine blessing?" "I do not know," was the reply from the gentleman whom he addressed; "but, if you please, sir, we will disappoint him on this occasion." And he rapped for silence among his friends, and introduced a prayer from Dr. Payson.

You will be delighted, perhaps surprised, to find what an element of power you have in social prayer. A skillful, prayerful pastor may weave the whole case of sorrow and trial before him, and the connected history of the family in which he is ministering, into the language of supplication, so appropriately and so affectionately, that, by the Lord's blessing, he will unite and elevate all the hearts around him to the heavenly throne in the spirit of submission and love. He may impersonate the natural language of the sufferers themselves, so as to awaken in them a tender and suitable feeling of trust, desire, gratitude, and submission to the divine love and wisdom. I have seen the whole company present thus lifted up in feeling and spirit, deeply impressed, instructed, and moved by the language of united supplication, probably far more effectively than they could have been by exhortations addressed directly to themselves.

---

[101] Edward Payson (1783-1827) was nicknamed, "praying Payson" because of his deep devotion to his Lord. Our little volume *Legacy of a Legend* is an apt introduction to this forgotten man of God.

Such employment of the blessed privilege of prayer is an important study. We should feel it as much a pastor's duty to pre-think his subjects and utterance in prayer, addressed to a heavenly mind, as his subjects for instruction addressed to the ear of man. I do not forget that the Holy Spirit has promised to teach us in that same hour, in our particular crisis and call, what we ought to say. But I am also aware that his presence and power are to prepare us for our work for Jesus as well as to accompany us therein. We ought never to be separate from the spirit of prayer or preaching. But we are to be cautious how we lay careless hands upon the ark of God, or fail to "seek him in due order."[102] A young man who felt himself immediately inspired to preach, and remonstrated against the delay and uselessness of a prescribed study, said to Bishop Griswold, "You know, bishop, that God has no need of man's wisdom. It is the foolishness of preaching which is to be made the wisdom of God." "Yes, I know that," said the old bishop; "but God has still less need of man's folly. Foolish preaching may be very far from the foolishness of preaching of which God speaks."[103]

I would urge you to the utmost careful preparation within your power for all your service, and for every service in the work of the Lord which you undertake, whether preaching, conversation, or prayer. Strive to maintain the spirit of prayer as a fundamental element of power for all your work, and carry it with you whithersoever and for whatsoever you may be called or sent.

V. Another very important element of power in your ministry will be THE CULTIVATION AND EXERCISE OF SYMPATHIZING EMOTIONS, AND CHEERFUL, HAPPY VIEWS OF PERSONS AND THINGS. To make yourselves rightly acceptable to others, is, to say the least, a vast help toward making yourselves really useful. It is our dispensation to carry many burdens which do not belong to us, and to relieve many sorrows which come upon us only in our office. In the midst of these, we have no time and no opportunity for melancholy, depression, or

---

[102] 1 Chronicles 15:13.
[103] 1 Corinthians 1:18.

discontent. We are the ministers of a cheerful Gospel, and we should be cheerful ministers of that Gospel. The language of complaint we must never indulge; still less the feeling of petulance, anger, or resentment. We can do nothing in our private work as pastors, if we allow a cold manner, or a morose or indifferent aspect. Life is peculiarly with us a divine dispensation and ministry. Our personal interests, our various family affairs, will compel attention as much from us as from other men. But we are as the ministers of Christ under a special divine guardianship, as peculiarly given to the work of the Lord. Our bread will be given to us, and our water will be sure. We are to be contented and cheerful. The language of complaint can never help us. The utterance or the feeling of mortification or disappointment relieves no sorrow, reveals our own weakness, and always exposes us to a just reproach. I may say to you that I had been in the ministry twenty-four years before I received for my pastoral work a salary sufficient to afford me what might have been considered a proper support for my family. I never made one question or complaint concerning it to the authorities of my congregations, nor did I ever leave a people upon the ground of personal dissatisfaction with my provision.

I would impress upon you, in all your domestic and personal relations, learn to take with thankfulness that which the Lord is pleased to give you; and illustrate your real dependence on his love in the cultivation of the habit of contentment and cheerfulness, that "blessing of the Lord which maketh rich, and addeth no sorrow therewith."[104] Go every where to increase the joys, and not to add to the distress of the people. Do not make yourselves burdens to your friends, and by no hints or representations exact more than is appointed you.

There is a power in such a deportment of cheerfulness, contentment, delicacy, and refinement in your relations as pastor, which will make all your labors among your people "as apples of gold in a net-work of silver."[105]

[104] Proverbs 10:22.
[105] Proverbs 25:11.

You may be "poor, yet making many rich; as having nothing, and yet possessing all things."[106] Your very entrance among the flock committed to you will be giving light; and all will learn to feel that they are always the happier for seeing and hearing you in your pastoral work for the honor of your gracious Lord.

VI. All these elements of power are, after all, to be considered by us but the instruments of the divine power. THE GRAND POWER OF YOUR WORK IS ALWAYS IN THE ATTENDING MINISTRY OF THE HOLY SPIRIT. You go forth as ministers of the New Testament—of the Spirit, not of the letter.[107] The Holy Ghost, who separates you for the work to which he has called you,[108] will be always with you.[109] He will take of the things of Christ, and show them unto you.[110] You may seek his presence with affectionate trust. He will make your words to be spirit and life in the hearts of those to whom you minister for him. It is the great privilege of your ministry to be permitted to speak the mind of the Spirit, and to say, in a loving, trusting heart, of all your work, "It seemeth good to the Holy Ghost and to us."[111]

We have been acquainted with men in the ministry who seemed to us to be filled with the Holy Ghost; whose aspect and walk in life appeared always enlightened by the Spirit; whose prayers and teaching seemed always to be moved and prompted by the Spirit of God; and whose presence with us in the day of suffering would have been welcomed as a direct visitation of divine power, peace, and love.

Such a man was James W. Alexander, of the Presbyterian Church in New York, who seemed to be always walking in the beauties of holiness and in the love of the Spirit. Often have I

---

[106] 2 Corinthians 6:10.
[107] 2 Corinthians 3:6; cf. Romans 2:29; 7:6.
[108] Acts 13:2.
[109] John 14:16.
[110] John 16:14,15.
[111] Acts 15:28.

said of him, when I am sick and dying, no man would be a more acceptable ministering visitor to me.

I have no more time to speak of this particular exhibition of power in our ministry. These are very distinct elements of a faithful pastor's power, though by no means all which might be considered. Let me earnestly press these upon your remembrance. Strive to live in the Spirit, to walk in the Spirit, to pray in the Spirit, to speak in the Spirit; so that, however successful you may be in your work for Jesus, the glory may be wholly given to that one Spirit, who, in a variety of ministrations, is the one abiding Teacher of the ransomed Church of God: "For I give you to understand that no man can say that Jesus is the Lord, but by the Holy Ghost."[112]

VII. With these suggestions upon the POWER of a pastor's work, I will close my attempt to aid and encourage you in a life of usefulness in the ministry by some suggestions upon the ATTAINMENTS which, through the blessing of God, may be permitted to reward and honor our efforts. We are never left without a blessing upon a faithful ministry for Christ. But the extent to which we are really prospered, and the variety of that divine blessing, it will be impossible for us to know within the limits of our present life. Some facts, however, are so clearly promised, and so readily perceived as we go on in our course, that we can not refuse our testimony to the Lord's faithfulness to us, nor doubt that he has graciously accepted our labors for his glory and his truth.

1. *We shall enjoy a degree of manifest success in our effort.* From the idea of success I shall not exclude a fair measure of outward prosperity and social comfort in our outward life. We may expect a fair and adequate provision for our proper wants; a reasonable measure of personal health; the many domestic comforts which fill our habitations; the respect and kindness of our fellow-men; the "many fathers

---

[112] 1 Corinthians 12:3.

and mothers, brothers and sisters,"[113] which have been included in the Lord's gracious promise and providence.

I have seen much of human society, in all the varied classes of social life; and I must give my testimony with fidelity, that no class of men are more uniformly welcomed with respect, cherished with affection, honored in general esteem, and made comfortable and contented in their various earthly relations in our country, than the faithful and upright ministers of the Gospel of Christ. This habitual result in my observation, so far from being diminished in the progress of years, was never more manifestly the characteristic and the general tribute of the people in this nation than it is in our day. The ministry of the churches of Jesus our Lord have their full share of respect, of power, of influence in all portions of our land; and, in the degree of their personal claims, are uniformly and every where acknowledged with reverence, and welcomed with general respect.[114]

I must further say that this feeling and habit, in all its local relations, is uniformly measured to individuals by their fidelity in their pastoral duties and relations. The preacher is spoken of with respect, according to an intelligent valuation of his personal talent and accomplishments, as a public agent, and not unfrequently with a severe criticism and examination. But the faithful pastor dwells as a father among his children in every Church, and every congregation and community. He is embedded in a living home, and remembered and thought of with an unchangeable regard and confidence.

The preacher will fade with age. The pastor grows brighter as he proceeds; still advancing in human esteem; bringing forth his fruit in old age; illustrating in a far higher measure the beautiful reflection of the aged hero of Greece:

---

[113] Mark 10:30.

[114] Tragically, in the opening years of the 21st century, this "reverence (and) general respect" for the clergy are now a very rare commodity. Ministerial unfaithfulness has been widely publicized and the general confidence in Gospel Ministers is very low. This ought not to be accepted as an irreversible fact, but should move each man to do what he can to maintain a good conscience in the sight of God and man.

"To the still grave retiring, as to rest;
My people blessing—by my people blest."

My young friends, this is success in the highest earthly degree. It is a life which gathers out of this world all that earth can give, and leaves to man no want which is unsupplied.

2. *Such a pastor receives actual seals of his ministry in the divine conversion of souls to Christ their Savior.* How sweetly Paul says to the Corinthians: "Ye may have ten thousand instructors. Ye have not many fathers. In Christ Jesus I have begotten you through the Gospel."[115] How precious is this bond between a faithful pastor and the child of God, who owes to his ministry the salvation of his own soul!

I am sure I shall never forget my sailor-boy, of whom I have already told you, as the first-fruits of my youthful ministry. Paul employs the figure, and I may also use it. I do not believe that any young mother rejoices over her first-born with a more real or a purer joy than a young Christian pastor rejoices over the first new-born soul, manifestly given to him as a sincere and loving minister of Jesus Christ.

I once heard a minister in middle age say that he did not know that God had ever given to him a single soul as a witness to his ministry. The utterance shocked me then long years ago, and it seems vastly more shocking to me now. What is the life of a minister of Christ worth, if no precious souls are recovered and saved by the exercise and outpouring of his love for Jesus? All the comforts and gains of earth would seem to me as nothing in this comparison. I should take up the retrospective complaint of Grotius and Selden[116] in such a barren review: "Vita agitur, operose nihil agendo"—"My life has been spent in laboriously doing nothing at all."

---

[115] 1 Corinthians 4:15.
[116] Hugo Grotius (1583-1647) was a Dutch legal scholar and natural law philosopher and John Selden (1584-1654) was an English jurist, legal antiquary and oriental scholar.

But we shall not be left thus desolate if we are sincere and faithful in the work committed to us. The residue of the spirit is with the Lord. He will never be slack in his promise, however longsuffering he may be toward us.[117] And how great will be the joy of looking upon those whom the Lord has given to us, as we are training them for him, and edifying them in his service, and in the anticipation of his glorious coming.

This is the real success of our life—winning souls for Jesus. It is a joy which no man taketh from us. And this is the peculiar result of a faithful pastoral work: feeding the sheep and the lambs of the Savior's flock. The more truly we are devoted to this one purpose of life, the more abundantly will he multiply his blessings upon us. If we strive, "in season, out of season,"[118] to lead ransomed souls to Jesus, hiding ourselves in the light which shines from him not preaching ourselves, but Jesus Christ the Lord[119]— "Of Zion it shall be said for us, that this and that man were born there;"[120] and "the Lord shall rehearse it when he writeth up his people;"[121] when "they that are wise shall shine as the brightness of the firmament, and they who turn many to righteousness, as the stars, forever and ever."[122]

3. *We may have the great joy of receiving special revivals of the Savior's work under our ministry.* Those great revivals which refreshed the churches of this country in former years can never be forgotten by the men who were permitted to labor in them. They were wonderful demonstrations of the presence and power of the Spirit of God in the Savior's Church on earth. I will give you some illustrations in a short account of two, in which my own ministry was personally occupied, and the influence and results of which I saw and knew.

---

[117] 2 Peter 3:9.
[118] 2 Timothy 4:2.
[119] 2 Corinthians 4:5.
[120] Psalm 87:5.
[121] Psalm 87:6.
[122] Daniel 12:3.

In the opening of the year 1820 I was in Bristol, Rhode Island, preparing for my ministry with the venerable Bishop Griswold. I have already referred to the Sabbath evening on which he officiated for the last time for two months. During all this period he was confined with a severe illness to his house. At our weekly prayer-meeting on the previous Friday evening, there were but thirteen persons present. It appeared to us a most depressing condition, and almost hopeless. On Monday, after the events before described, there appeared a very remarkable earnestness and interest among the people, manifested in conversation among little gatherings around, and resulting in a general demand for an assembling of the people for a religious worship and conference. They were unwilling to wait for the regular meeting of Friday. Accordingly, a meeting was privately notified to be held in a private house offered for the purpose on Thursday evening. It became my duty to conduct it. I found the house at the appointed time as completely filled as it would have been at a crowded funeral.

A small table was placed for me on the half-way landing of the stairs, with a Bible and a hymn-book; and there I stood, in all the weakness of a youth not twenty years of age, to address an anxious assembly, filling every space which I could see, and the rooms which were beyond my sight. That meeting was the commencement of a series of nightly public meetings, which were continued for three months. These were also soon connected with the appointment of another in the afternoon, and then another in the morning, of most of the days in different parts of the town, and in many of the country dwellings around. The same awakened spirit was found in the Methodist and Presbyterian churches. We worked together in unison and harmony. The whole population of the town seemed to feel the solemn impulse. The business of the people was for a season arrested. The stores were closed. The general interest of the people appeared to be consecrated to the one great thought and purpose of the soul's salvation.

I have not time to dwell upon the incidents of this wonderful season. Many of them were very remarkable. And I can not speak personally beyond the experience of the Episcopal Church. There seemed to be scarce a person in the town unaffected or uninterested in the one great theme of conversation. There were some scoffers; but they awakened no thought on their side. The whole work was too manifestly the work of the Lord to be derided.

Perhaps eight weeks had passed by, during which, in outward ministry, I was quite alone in the Episcopal Church to meet this whole aggregate of demand for public teaching and private conference. When the bishop, who was also the rector of the church, became sufficiently restored to receive a number at his house, sixty or seventy of the new converts were assembled in his dining-room. Sitting in his chair, a manifest invalid, he addressed these precious souls. You may readily conceive how my young heart rejoiced at the sight, and in the sound of his encouraging voice.

I was laboring there in the same way, not with the same increasing numbers, for a full year after this occasion. There was no diminution of religious interest, and not much more in public services; no retraction of earnestness in the persons thus converted, nor in the general effects produced. This was a revival; the work of the Spirit of God; the fruit and the result of the truly faithful pastoral ministry and public teaching of the venerable man of God to whom I have referred, who had been for near twenty years the beloved pastor of that church. How much I learned of the appointed work and blessing of the ministry during that period you can readily see. It was the beginning of my life, and it left an unchangeable impression on my ministry. I speak of the whole event here as one of the blessed attainments of the ministry through the gift of the Holy Spirit.

In the winter of 1831, in the city of Philadelphia, God was pleased to open to me another similar manifestation of his grace. Our weekly prayer-meeting was on Saturday evening. At the close of the meeting on this occasion, after I had dismissed the assembly, sixteen persons of both sexes, all youthful, remained on their knees in different parts of the room, unconscious of each other's presence. I went round and spoke to each. I knelt and prayed with all. And after another hour thus spent they retired. I was overwhelmed with gratitude and amazement.

On the Sabbath morning succeeding, I gave some account of the preceding evening, and appointed a meeting on Monday evening for conversation with all who were awakened to seek their personal salvation. At that meeting more than seventy persons came under this invitation. I have already referred to this meeting in a previous lecture. This was the commencement of a very remarkable revival. During two years succeeding, in all the seasons, we maintained a morning prayer-meeting daily at six o'clock, which even in mid-winter was well attended.

The immediate results of this divine visitation were in the conversion of more than two hundred persons, among whom were fifteen married couples in the early maturity of life. Some of the incidents and individual cases of conversion during this gracious season were as remarkable and peculiar as any of which I have ever heard. I have already referred to a few of these, and I have not time to dwell too long upon others.

A very fashionable lady, the wife of a Commodore in the navy, was, with her husband and family, a portion of my congregation. At our early prayer-meeting in winter, on one Thursday morning, this lady was present, and waited for me at the close of the meeting, and I accompanied her to her house. I will give you the account, as nearly as I can, in her own words. She said:

"I have not been in bed during the whole night. I have left my husband and children asleep; and after having walked the floor the whole night, I remembered your meeting at six o'clock, and locked my street door, and came to meet you here. Last evening I was coming down Walnut

Street, after dark, on my return to my home. When opposite to Washington Square, I heard a church bell ringing. I felt an irresistible impulse, I know not why, to follow the sound. I saw a number of persons going into a church of which I had no knowledge, and I followed them. They ascended the stairs leading to a lecture-room over the hall, and I accompanied them, and sat down. Presently I saw you come in, and go into the desk. I was amazed. I know not what influence it was, but you preached to me as I never heard you before. My whole soul was aroused. I longed to speak to you after the service was concluded; but I hesitated until you were gone, and I went home alone. And now I have come to you this morning for your instruction and guidance."

You may imagine with what astonishment I listened to this recital. At my tea-table the preceding evening a gentleman called to say that Mr. Barnes,[123] the pastor of the church which she described, was suddenly ill, and to beg me to supply his place in his regular weekly lecture. I assented to his request, and went immediately, and this was the result.

The message of Peter to Cornelius hardly appeared to me more wonderful. The conversion of this lady was most entire—a wonderful illustration of grace. She honored her Savior in a faithful life, and in a subsequent happy departure. But this was only one of many instances of the all-sufficient grace of a glorified Savior which were witnessed in that revival.

Of such revivals of the actual influence of the Gospel, as distinct blessings from Jesus to his Church, I can not speak but as of gifts of grace of the highest worth, and as attainments for the ministry of the utmost value and importance. For such the faithful pastors of his people will earnestly labor. For them all the living members of his Church should pray and strive. The language of his prophet

---

[123] Albert Barnes (1798-1870) was an American pastor and theologian who was pastor of First Presbyterian Church of Philadelphia from 1830-1867.

should be the utterance of their hearts: "O Lord, revive thy work in the midst of the years; in wrath remember mercy."[124]

4. *In the pursuit of such a pastoral ministry as I have sketched, there will be found much HAPPINESS as a sure attainment for the faithful servant of the Lord Jesus.* The labors of the Christian ministry are in themselves an unspeakable privilege; and they confer unceasing pleasure upon the man whose heart is in his work. The daily dealing with those who love the work of the Lord; the unceasing ministration of comfort and peace to the weary; the removing of burdens from the heavy laden; the permission to give our whole time to the work of the Lord upon the earth; to see our personal efforts constantly promoting comfort and strength to others—can not but afford the purest comfort to a generous and loving spirit.

There is a pleasure in the public proclamation of the Word of God when we are made successful in awakening attention, and in communicating religious instruction and elevated motives and purposes to others, which can not be transcended by the enjoyment of any other life of man on earth. For mere intellectual enjoyment, perhaps the public duties of the pulpit may be to the minister of Christ the source of a higher or more exhilarating satisfaction; but the daily faithful work of the Christian pastor ministers to himself a calm, pure, and unceasing gratification. I am perfectly sure that no class of men attain a more tranquil, contented, or really satisfied mind than they who have cheerfully given their whole thought and time and faithful care to the one work of rescuing from evil, of recalling to duty, of elevating in holiness, both by their instruction and their example, the multitude of their fellow-men—bought with the same precious blood, and called by the same Divine Spirit—to the same heavenly and eternal home of a reconciled Father and God.

---

[124] Habakkuk 3:2.

And when you add to all this the final retrospect of life and the glorious hope with which it closes, how filled with satisfaction is such a remembrance, and how abounding in happiness has been such a career.

The eminent Archbishop Williams said in his dying hour, "I have filled more places of trust in Church and State than any man before me in this kingdom. But in this hour I should have more satisfaction in knowing that I had been the instrument of bringing one soul to Christ my Lord, than I can now take in all the honor and wealth which I have enjoyed on earth."

But when you pass beyond this retrospect of earthly life to the living testimony of the divine acceptance and favor, and anticipate that last acknowledgment of a faithful pastor's work—"Well done, good and faithful servant; enter thou into the joy of thy Lord"[125]—how complete becomes the recompense of your work! How satisfying is the choice which you have made! How thoroughly remunerative has been the investment of all the powers of your life and being in this one work, whatever you may have had to give, and whatever it may have really cost you.

I thus complete the course which I was desired to address to you, my young friends, in these five lectures. I entered upon the task with no reluctance, though not without inconvenience at my advanced period of life. If I have really succeeded in gratifying, encouraging, and instructing you, the remembrance of our meeting here will be a pleasure to me amid the many cares of a declining and closing day, and the many obligations and burdens which in the providence of my gracious Lord still remain upon me.

And with much gratitude for the attention and respect with which I have been received and welcomed, I offer you my best wishes and my earnest prayer for your full success in all the work of life, and your final acceptance and reward from your gracious Master's hands.

THE END

---

[125] Matthew 25:21,23.

# A
# Scriptural
# Index

# Other Solid Ground Titles

In addition to the book in your hand, Solid Ground is honored to offer other uncovered treasure, many for the first time in more than a century:

NOTES ON GALATIANS by J. Gresham Machen

EXPOSITION OF THE BAPTIST CATECHISM by Benjamin Beddome

PAUL THE PREACHER: *Sermons from Acts* by John Eadie

THE COMMUNICANT'S COMPANION by Matthew Henry

THE CHILD AT HOME by John S.C. Abbott

THE LIFE OF JESUS CHRIST FOR THE YOUNG by Richard Newton

THE KING'S HIGHWAY: *10 Commandments for the Young* by Richard Newton

HEROES OF THE REFORMATION by Richard Newton

FEED MY LAMBS: *Lectures to Children on Vital Subjects* by John Todd

LET THE CANNON BLAZE AWAY by Joseph P. Thompson

THE STILL HOUR: *Communion with God in Prayer* by Austin Phelps

COLLECTED WORKS of James Henley Thornwell (4 vols.)

CALVINISM IN HISTORY *by Nathaniel S. McFetridge*

OPENING SCRIPTURE: *Hermeneutical Manual by Patrick Fairbairn*

THE ASSURANCE OF FAITH *by Louis Berkhof*

THE PASTOR IN THE SICK ROOM *by John D. Wells*

THE BUNYAN OF BROOKLYN: *Life & Sermons of I.S. Spencer*

THE NATIONAL PREACHER: *Sermons from 2nd Great Awakening*

FIRST THINGS: *First Lessons God Taught Mankind Gardiner Spring*

BIBLICAL & THEOLOGICAL STUDIES *by 1912 Faculty of Princeton*

THE POWER OF GOD UNTO SALVATION *by B.B. Warfield*

THE LORD OF GLORY *by B.B. Warfield*

A GENTLEMAN & A SCHOLAR: *Memoir of J.P. Boyce by J. Broadus*

SERMONS TO THE NATURAL MAN *by W.G.T. Shedd*

SERMONS TO THE SPIRITUAL MAN *by W.G.T. Shedd*

HOMILETICS AND PASTORAL THEOLOGY *by W.G.T. Shedd*

A PASTOR'S SKETCHES 1 & 2 *by Ichabod S. Spencer*

THE PREACHER AND HIS MODELS *by James Stalker*

IMAGO CHRISTI: *The Example of Jesus Christ by James Stalker*

LECTURES ON THE HISTORY OF PREACHING *by J. A. Broadus*

THE SHORTER CATECHISM ILLUSTRATED *by John Whitecross*

THE CHURCH MEMBER'S GUIDE *by John Angell James*

THE SUNDAY SCHOOL TEACHER'S GUIDE *by John A. James*

CHRIST IN SONG: *Hymns of Immanuel from All Ages by Philip Schaff*

DEVOTIONAL LIFE OF THE S.S. TEACHER *by J.R. Miller*

Call us Toll Free at 1-877-666-9469
Send us an e-mail at sgcb@charter.net
Visit us on line at solid-ground-books.com
*Uncovering Buried Treasure to the Glory of God*

Printed in the United States
46781LVS00001B/103-204

9 781599 250557